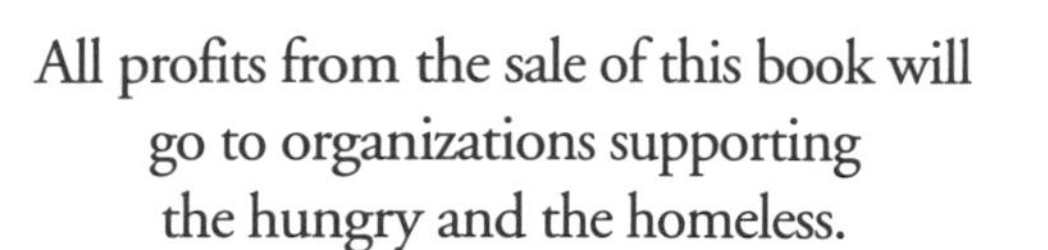

All profits from the sale of this book will
go to organizations supporting
the hungry and the homeless.

Your purchase donation will go to:

**A Special Thanks to the Community Soup Kitchen
and Liberty Community Services ... New Haven, Connecticut.**

DINNER AT SIX:

VOICES FROM THE SOUP KITCHEN

by Helen Hudson

published by

Wildfire Press

Email: Wildfirepress@aol.com

Published by Wildfire Press.
Wildfirepress@aol.com

Hudson, Helen

Dinner at six: Voices from the Soup Kitchen / Helen Hudson

ISBN 0-9631537-1-4

Fifth Printing — May 2006

Cover Photography/Design: Loy Whitman

Book design: www.parkerdesignstudio.com

Published in the United States of America

2 3 4 5 6

To the Guests

who had the courage

to live these lives

and to tell me

their stories.

"Let them know we want to work."
— Ray

"Tell them we're not bad people."
— Josie

TABLE OF CONTENTS

PREFACE

This work grew out of my experience as a volunteer in a group of evening soup kitchens known as the Center City Soup Kitchens (CCSK). The name is fictitious as are all proper names of persons and places. The main body of the work consists of a series of interviews with some of the guests (the accepted term for people served in soup kitchens.) There are many excellent scholarly works on the very poor and the homeless, studies that describe them, analyze them, count them and categorize them — by age, sex, nationality, class and even "underclass." My focus is on the individuals — who they are, where they came from, what brought them to the soup kitchen, how they feel about it, how they see themselves and how they cope with the extreme hardships and humiliations they are forced to endure. The interviews were open-ended. I simply let the interviewees tell the story of their lives in their own way with very few interruptions from me. I have, however, edited the taped material by cutting, in some cases extensively, and rearranging it in order to give each life story a logical structure and coherence.

The book includes a general introduction which gives some information about CCSK: its organization, my role in it, how this project originated and how the interviews were conducted. This is followed by a section on "The Volunteers" and one on the "Guests." "The Kitchen" is a composite picture of an evening at a soup kitchen, describing the procedure, the food, the behavior of the people involved and the general atmosphere.

The main section, "The Voices," consists of fifteen interviews. The "Epilogue" gives a brief follow-up on some of the guests. Most have disappeared.

THE BACKGROUND

INTRODUCTION

The hand-printed sign outside the parish house announced "Soup Kitchen Tonight, 6–7." It was moved each day from church to church in the very center of the city among the pompous public buildings around the Green: the Library, the Court House, the Town Hall, the banks and the neo-Gothic intrusions of Carlyle University — symbols of wealth, power and prestige, perched on the edge of the ghetto. I passed that sign twice every day on my way to and from the University library where I go to write, and saw clumps of shabby people standing outside the locked doors. If they were early, they would have to wait in the cold and the heat and the rain and the snow. If they were late, the food might all be gone. Since I live in the center of town where the homeless tend to congregate, I saw them often. They were mostly young African American men, pushing grocery carts piled high, not with groceries but with empty bottles and cans; selling newspapers on windy corners; sifting through trash cans; standing in shop doorways with paper cups, asking those who hurry by for spare change, an echo of the song of the thirties, "Brother, can you spare a dime?"

I saw them in the early morning after the shelters had closed, walking down dark streets but going nowhere, carrying their worldly goods in plastic shopping bags. For the homeless must take their belongings with them like permanent refugees. They have lost their homes but do not, like victims of natural disasters or terrorist attacks, qualify for emergency relief. In fact, the word "homeless" was rarely mentioned in public or in the media in the years before the bombs fell on the World Trade Center. Yet the soup kitchens were crowded long before that attack and the shelters were full and forced to turn people away. But when politicians mentioned the poor, they were always careful to define them as *working* families, as if the unemployed and the homeless were not worthy even of lip service. Poor children were, of course, of great concern. But what about their parents? Dubbed by the demeaning term "underclass," they are not merely relegated to the bottom of society, they have been pushed out completely, taking their children with them. Their voices are never heard in public. They are not only as invisible as parking meters but as mute as well. Except that the homeless are forever walking — from the shelter to the soup kitchen, to the Welfare office, to the clinic, to the library, buildings that are far apart. In the end, it is back to the single room or the shelter or the street.

The sign outside the parish house had a message for me as well and I became a volunteer with CCSK (Central City Soup Kitchen). This is supported by four Protestant churches which house seven kitchens in four different locations. The entire operation was in the hands of Harper, the Director (only first names are used in the soup kitchens as now in society at large). Harper is a tall, pleasant African American in jeans and cap who enjoys good relations with both guests and volunteers. He is also capable and conscientious, assisted only by Nan and Ted, two hard-working, part-time staff members who mingle easily with the guests. Much of the work is done by volunteers.

The basements where the dinners are served have large rooms with kitchens attached and movable furniture. At St. Peter's, there are toys piled up at one end with an upright piano beside them. The walls are hung with lines from the Lord's Prayer, written in wobbly, childish letters that threaten to fall off the page. This room, like others in which the soup kitchens are held, was obviously used as a nursery school during the day. How many of the children who play there in the morning, I wondered, would, some day, come back in the evening to stand on line at the other end of the room.

The majority of our guests are African American men with a sprinkling of Hispanics and a small number of Whites, though this last group is increasing. There are some women from all three groups but mostly African Americans, and a few children. Ages range predominantly from the late twenties through the forties. The elderly do not like to come out in the dark and the cold, and the teenagers rebel. "My daughter loved the soup kitchen when she was younger," one guest reported, "but now she's older, it's like she's ashamed to come." Some come regularly, some occasionally, some for only a short time. Many disappear for a period and then return. When this happens, the reappearing guest usually gets a warm welcome. Many leave for good. To go where? To another town in search of work? To the hospital? To prison? To the grave? There are always others to take their place.

In the beginning, the guests were merely anonymous figures to me. They came out of the night and went back into the night. After a while, the long line of indistinguishable shapes became individual people with unique faces and personalities. I learned the names of many — as they learned mine — and even something about them.

My main job in the soup kitchen was to take a count each night of the guests (just numbers, not names). But, like most volunteers, I helped with anything that needed to be done: prepared the food for serving, helped serve it when we were short-handed and helped in the cleaning up afterwards.

As the recordkeeper, I stood at the head of the table which gave me a good chance to talk to the guests while they waited to be served or in the lull between "firsts" and "seconds" or for longer discussions after dinner as some tended to linger at the serving table on their way out.

After a while, my contacts extended beyond the walls of the soup kitchen. I often met guests on my errands around town. I met them on the street, gathered in the Mall — for warmth, not shopping — sitting on the Green or in Columbus Park, the small park opposite my house, or in the public library, watching video tapes or reading newspapers and magazines, even working on computers. In the free public library, at least, I thought, they could be warm and comfortable. In the free public library — the most egalitarian place in town — they are treated like other members of the public, though with no permanent address, it was more difficult for them to obtain membership cards. Even in the most democratic of institutions, the homeless are not entirely equal.

Their greetings to me are extremely friendly, anywhere from a hug or a "Hi, Helen," shouted from across the Green, to the tipping of caps and parka hoods. I even meet them in the supermarket early in the morning after the shelters have closed. They stand with their smiles and their paper cups of coffee while I greet them with considerable embarrassment, from behind an overloaded shopping cart.

I tried not to think about their lives beyond the soup kitchen. What is it like to have no job, no money, no home, no permanent bed or no bed at all? How does it feel to be forced to beg for "loose change" or to rummage through other people's garbage? I wondered why they did not seem to feel any resentment toward us, the comfortable middle class. I thought of the large, white woman in a huge skirt like a bedspread, a man's hat, little white socks and sneakers, who always sits on the same bench on the Green and asks for 35 cents for the bus.

"But the fare has gone up," I say.

"The Lord will provide," she says with folded hands.

I thought of the young man who stands patiently outside an abandoned building with his empty cup. "God bless you," he says when I drop my donation into his cup. It is what he always says.

"He already has," I say. It is what I always say, in an embarrassed mumble. I was even more embarrassed when I had to explain to the guests why I disappeared for four months every summer which we spend in our flat in England, revealing that I had two homes when they had none. Yet they always greeted me warmly on my first night back. "Hi! How was England?" I had read several articles on why the poor don't hate the rich and, while the arguments seemed convincing on the page, I am still surprised and puzzled when I meet the phenomenon in person.

Driving some of the guests home at night, I had a chance for longer conversations. I also helped out at the Downtown Recreation Center, known as the Rec Center, held in the basement of the First Congregational Church on Wednesday afternoons, run by Harper with assistance from the staff and a few volunteers. This offers refreshments, lectures and information given by experts on matters of interest to our guests such as: Legal Aid, Health Care, Mental Health, Drug Treatment Programs, Employment and aid in writing resumés. For entertainment there are board games, secondhand books donated by Ted, a staff member, from his secondhand bookshop, and music, sometimes performed by professionals, sometimes by the guests themselves, and even a raffle. Ted introduced a poster painting project to cover the walls of a huge, grim-looking, abandoned building in the center of town. He also initiated a Cabaret and helped the guests develop their acts which they then performed for the Wednesday night soup kitchen. These included songs, guitar recitals, poetry, written and read by the guests, stand-up comics and anything else a guest wished to present.

At first I signed up for one night a week. Quite soon I was going two, then three, then five nights a week. I increased my hours for several reasons: I was needed, I was interested, and I found the liveliness and camaraderie that often prevailed in the soup kitchens exhilarating. In short, I enjoyed it.

After I'd been working there for over two years and was quite a familiar figure to most of the guests, I decided to try some interviews. I was curious to know more about them and I thought that, if things went well, I might turn the material into a book, though I certainly had no assurance that this would happen and no clear idea of the form the book might take. But I did know that I wanted to give our guests a chance to tell their stories to a hostile or, at best, an indifferent world.

I was extremely apprehensive. I knew nothing about interviewing; I didn't even know how to operate a tape recorder (though the guests were very helpful in teaching me!). Moreover, such an undertaking seemed like prying. It was intrusive, even offensive, made worse by the fact that I had no academic standing and that I am a white, middle-class woman and most of my interviewees would be extremely poor African American men. It seemed to me that I represented the enemy and they the victims. How would they react to my invasion of their privacy?

I need not have worried. They were surprisingly open about themselves but never asked me any personal questions. Except for a cheery "How was England?"

I explained to the guests that I would like to interview them about their lives, past and present; that I was interested in learning how they happened to come to the soup kitchen, and how they were living and coping; a project that might, or might not, grow into a book. I assured them that I would use pseudonyms. To my great surprise, almost no one turned me down. Most saw it as a way of helping the homeless, as an opportunity to put their case to the uninformed public.

"Let them know we *want* to work," Ray said.

"Tell them we're not bad people," Josie said.

In the end, I had more interviews than I could use.

We had to find convenient public places where we could meet with some privacy during the day. This put an extra burden on the guests who already spent so much of their time traveling around the city. They had no telephones, which was awkward as we had no way of getting in touch with each other except at the soup kitchen. They accepted all this cheerfully and came quite faithfully in all kinds of weather. To my surprise, most were more or less prompt, though few had watches and there are, virtually, no public clocks in town.

We used several places. One of the churches kindly allowed us to meet in its very attractive lounge once a week and the public library gave us the use of an empty office. These were ideal: warm, comfortable, quiet, private and well located for the guests. Matt got a part-time job in a parking lot during the course of our interviews and we carried on in his little booth where there was a heater, a coffee pot and only occasional interruptions from his customers and street friends.

Less satisfactory was a small storeroom in one of the churches which was open one afternoon a week for the Rec Center. The storeroom was cold and crowded with dirty mops, brooms, pails, rags and boxes of miscellaneous equipment. It included a rickety, food-stained highchair for the tape recorder and two hard, folding chairs which we managed to squeeze in for ourselves. It was also very noisy with constant loud sounds from the Rec Center: a guitar, a piano, singing, shouting, laughter and loud applause.

The interviews were a great surprise. People seemed to enjoy the opportunity to talk about their lives and did so with amazing vividness. Quite a few seemed to have almost total recall. They spoke openly about their mistakes, their failures, their crimes. Some of the interviews went on for many hours, even over several days. They spoke, not only with remarkable candor but, even more surprising, without much bitterness except about the proposed welfare cuts, the second within two years. Many seemed bewildered, some ashamed at what had happened to them and blamed themselves as well as that vague, impersonal force, the economy. Only a very few expressed any resentment toward politics or the social system, though racism, in one form or another, was often mentioned.

Almost all the people interviewed here showed remarkable resilience and faced their situation with courage and even with optimism and humor. And they asked for so little — a home and a job. I have tried to let them speak for themselves in the hope that there are some who will be willing to listen.

THE VOLUNTEERS

The kitchens depend heavily on volunteers. Their numbers change with the weather and the seasons. Some are students from high schools, colleges and graduate schools in the area. Many are Carlyle University undergraduates who live in college buildings close to the soup kitchens. They are, predictably, a floating population. Few come for more than a year, though some of the graduate students come faithfully until they receive their degrees. All disappear during the holidays, leaving the kitchens very short-handed.

The older volunteers — some of whom have been coming for years — include church members, social workers, teachers, office workers, a clergyman, a lawyer, a businessman, a computer expert and assorted concerned citizens. Sometimes they are joined by people from Workfare and Community Services.* Lester, a volunteer, shows up every Thursday to play the piano during dinner, which gives the place a festive air.

Volunteers vary greatly in their commitment. Most agree to work one

* Community Service involves part-time work for petty crimes in lieu of a jail sentence. Workfare is work required of all Welfare recipients, usually low level, unskilled jobs.

night a week. Some come faithfully year after year, some come for a year or two, some only a few times. One woman who turned up as a volunteer for the first time, became ecstatic at the sight of "so many doing the work of the Lord," as if He had provided the homeless for just that purpose. She never came again.

Volunteers vary a good deal in their performance as well. Some, especially students, come barely in time to serve and leave as soon as the serving is over. Others come early to help with preparations and a few stay late to help clean up. Estelle, a middle-aged woman in a long apron and rubber gloves, spends the evening with her head in the kitchen sink scrubbing trays and pots and pans. Dick, a computer expert, comes faithfully every week straight from his office, after the kitchen is closed, to do the heavy work of sweeping and mopping. Some of the guests usually help with the cleaning up.

Some volunteers insist on enforcing the kitchen's rules regardless of any special circumstances; rules such as only one packet of salt per person; no extra portions to be taken home to sick wives or children even when the food is plentiful and the turnout poor; no money to be given to the guests. Others are more flexible — or more humane. Still others play favorites. Some volunteers thoughtlessly help themselves to food before the guests arrive though there is often a danger that there will not be enough.

All volunteers are polite to the guests, addressing them as "Sir" or "Miss." But many show little interest in them and prefer to spend the evening talking to each other, even while serving. I wonder if Estelle chooses to keep her head in the sink in order to avoid any contact with the guests. Rhoda wears a long smock, like a hospital gown, that covers all of her as if to protect her from all possible contamination. Sylvia, a member of a host church, is a square, high-shouldered woman with a sharp crease in her trousers and between her eyes. She is extremely hard-working but has a stern, moralistic attitude toward the guests. Martha, an attractive woman in her fifties, in well-cut trousers (never jeans) and hand-knitted sweaters (never T-shirts), rarely smiles and maintains an impersonal attitude toward the guests. She gives the impression that she is merely doing her Christian duty — which she does very well. She always comes early and stays late, and is conscientious and efficient. But she might as well be feeding the ducks.

Others seem more aware of the people they are serving and do more than simply fill their plates. Brian jokes with the guests as they come down the line and knows many of them by name. Martin, a retired teacher, has a pleasant jovial manner towards everyone — guests and volunteers alike — and the atmosphere grows brighter and warmer when he appears. Norman is a long-time volunteer who is silent and business-like when serving but makes a point of hiring guests to do odd jobs such as washing his car and painting his kitchen. Kate works two nights a week and is willing to do anything that needs to be done, including putting in extra hours during the holidays. She knows many of the guests by name and often, when she is not needed to serve, sits down and drinks coffee with them. When she saw Muriel, a homeless guest, wandering around in her neighborhood, she invited her in for tea.

Nan, a staff member, had allowed Rodney, who had lost a leg in a car accident, to use her home as a mailing address. She was helping him to get legal advice on collecting insurance for this when he was killed crossing the street on a rainy morning. Nan wrote a moving obituary for him which was printed in the local newspaper and read aloud by Harper at the Tuesday night soup kitchen.

Interaction among the volunteers and staff varies, too. Some volunteers show no interest in their fellow workers and tend to remain aloof. The students talk mainly to each other. But there is usually a corps of steady volunteers (and staff) who have been working together for several years and talk and joke in the kitchen as they prepare the food or clean up afterward. This includes any guests who may be helping.

I often see Nan, Ted, Kate and Brian at demonstrations and meetings pertaining to the homeless and we have become friends outside the soup kitchen. But whenever we meet, some part of our talk is always connected, in some way, with the soup kitchen. We find, as others undoubtedly have, that working there is an intense and rewarding experience.

THE GUESTS

Our guests come from the north and the south, from cities and farms. Some travel constantly in search of jobs and cheap housing or better shelters, hoping, as Josie does, to "start over." "Seems like I've spent my whole life moving and being moved," Ralph says. But they are rootless, rather than the disparaging term "drifters," for they have been uprooted. They represent various stages of homelessness and many move from one to the other. Some have experienced them all, for all stages are highly precarious. Some live, on and off, crowded in with family members or friends. A very few live in apartments but cannot afford to buy food; some live in single rooms in the Y or in rooming houses with other Welfare recipients. Often they live two in a room. These rooms have communal bathrooms and no cooking facilities. Some, in this harrowing journey between a room and the street, sleep in shelters. One cannot say they *live* there for they are thrown out at 7:30 in the morning, regardless of the weather and must stay out until late afternoon when they have to line up early to be sure of a bed for the night. If you "live" in a shelter, you don't even have the same bed every night. If the shelter is crowded or closed, you have no bed at all. People in shelters have no place to store their belongings but must carry them around with them. Some, when evicted, are forced to put everything but their personal belongings in storage. When they can no longer keep up the payments, they lose it all.

Even those with jobs are sometimes forced to sleep in shelters or eat in soup kitchens because they cannot earn enough to pay for rent or food. Since low rentals are in dangerous, drug-infested neighborhoods where crimes of all kinds, including murder, are common; some prefer to spend all their money on rent and eat in the soup kitchens. A few of our guests literally live on the street. (The British, in a vivid phrase, call it "sleeping rough.") A very few prefer it to the shelters which are noisy and crowded and where they may be robbed or attacked. Some have no choice.

"Still," Kenneth says, "if you're homeless, you can live anywhere — on any street. If you have no job and no family, you have no responsibilities. You can always start over again somewhere else," as many try to do. Relationships shift easily. Friends disappear, couples break up, new ones are formed. Homelessness breeds restlessness.

And it breeds promiscuity. For people who have no home, the temptation to go wherever there is a roof and a bed must be irresistible. Sleeping around becomes a way of life. Spike has lived, on and off, with several women for years. Josie and Deirdre have lived on the street and with various men who offered them refuge. But these arrangements are often brief and sometimes end in disaster with unwanted pregnancies, robberies and beatings.

For homelessness is, among other things, dangerous — beginning with the constant threat of the police. Ironically, the homeless, who have almost nothing, are often robbed of the little they have: Welfare checks, a few belongings, their backpacks. Derek was beaten and robbed while selling newspapers on the street. Kenneth has been robbed many times and was beaten right outside the door of a shelter in New York with a crowd looking on. Marshall was mugged and robbed inside the Y. Women, especially, are in danger — from roommates or strangers. Deirdre, a small, white woman often arrives in the soup kitchen with some part of her bruised or broken. Muriel, a permanent street dweller, was attacked and robbed of the few clothes I had given her. One night I learned that her homeless boyfriend, Mick, had been murdered.

Homeless people seem remarkably generous about sharing their "homes" — when they have one. Josie invited homeless friends to live with her several times, sometimes with unfortunate results.

Many grew up in poverty and its companion, broken homes. Leeta, speaking of the several fathers of her children, says, "Maybe you used to find somebody who would stick by you, help you financially. But now seems like everybody's just out for theirselves." Many grew up without fathers, some without mothers. "You've got to be really fortunate to have a father that stays with you," James said. Ralph's father disappeared before he was born and he was removed from his mother by the State (she was a barmaid and considered unfit), dooming him to a series of orphanages and foster homes.

Matt and Spike had stepfathers they hated and mothers who were indifferent, even negligent. Gordon grew up in a middle-class home with both parents but his father was cold and unforgiving and his mother seems to have been unwilling or unable to protect him. Michelle, when a girl, was repeatedly raped by her grandfather. Her grandmother insisted it was Michelle's fault.

Violence was, quite often, a routine occurrence: at home, in the neighborhood and at school. Hughie's father beat his wife and children whenever he came home. Spike was repeatedly beaten by his stepfather and was never protected by his mother. Ralph suffered violence and sexual abuse in some of his foster homes. Others reported that corporal punishment was a regular feature of family life.

Violence was common in the neighborhood as well. Matt, a white boy in a white neighborhood, had to fight every day for months after he moved in because he was a "newcomer." Curtis, at fifteen, was beaten half to death by a gang of African American boys, neighbors and classmates, because his skin "was lighter than the other boys."

But, for many, school was the main area of violence. Some were beaten by their teachers: Michelle by her African American teachers in the South, Mark by his Muslim teachers in New York. Ralph, who spent part of his boyhood in a Catholic orphanage, was subjected to cruel punishments by the nuns for trivial misdeeds. Gordon went to a Catholic school where the nuns beat the children for any slight infraction. "We had the highest suicide rate in the city," he said.

The worst offenders, however, were the students themselves. Lonnie's school in South Carolina had just been integrated and the Whites and Blacks fought each other three or four times a day. Todd, in New Hope, reported that as soon as the school bus was parked, everyone got off and fought. Mark's school in New York was the scene of constant and extremely brutal warfare among students wielding bats, knives and guns. "It was a school for crime, not learning," Mark says. He, like others, dropped out — without a diploma and without any skills.

In spite of this, many of the unskilled as well as the skilled were able to find jobs as long as the economy was fairly sound. "Used to be I could get work any time, doing anything, because I'm a fast learner," Seth reported. But this is no longer true. "I never had any trouble getting a job until the recession set in," Eric, an industrial engineer, said. "I had four main interests in my life: engineering, art, music and cooking, and I was fairly successful in all of them. But, in the end, they didn't lead anywhere — except to the soup kitchen."

Some are sick or disabled — the cause or the consequence of extreme poverty? Several, during the winters, are in and out of hospitals with pneumonia and other debilitating ailments.

A few are unable to work because of permanent physical disabilities. One young man has only one arm, another one leg. Some became disabled in the service, some by accidents on the job or by incurable diseases: severe arthritis, degenerative spinal condition, undiagnosed stomach ailment. Curtis, who was injured at work, is held together with a rod and wires and is often in pain. Spike has a bad leg from an accident on a construction site. Eric has severe arthritis in his hands and feet.

A few told me that they have AIDS, some that they are addicted to drugs or alcohol to which they were introduced by older relatives or friends, or by the military. They said this quite openly in the soup kitchen or during the interviews. All complain that they must wait for long periods to get into a treatment program. Some are cured of their addiction and stay cured. But others, thrown back into the same hopeless situation of joblessness and poverty and even homelessness, revert and must begin the whole process all over again — a process without progress.

Ex-convicts, too, have difficulty in finding jobs, even in good times. "I got out of prison like most people with a positive attitude," Hughie says. "Start looking for a job. You don't find none. Then back to the same old pattern."

A few have mental problems. Al, a Green Beret Vietnam veteran, a professional soldier and a hard-working volunteer, suffers from PTSD (Post Traumatic Stress Disorder). Kenneth, a classical pianist, had his life completely disrupted by a severe mental condition. Untreated, he was driven to living in the street for years while his condition grew increasingly worse. Sidney, an elderly white man, who suffers from some mental disturbance, says he hates the nights and hates himself. "I bang my head against the wall when there's too much darkness," he said. Adrian disappears periodically. "I went to the hospital," he explains. "I always get depressed in the spring."

For some, there is simply no place in our society. Walter, an elderly, white man who reads very widely in many fields and in several languages, is unable to find a job. Forced to leave college because of his family's economic problems, he does not have the degrees necessary for an academic post. And though he put himself through a business course, he never learned to run a computer. There is no place for him except in the University library where he spends his days reading widely in five languages which gives him a great deal of pleasure — but no income.

Given the grim circumstances of their present lives, the past, for some, takes on a rosy glow. James says of Montgomery Avenue, in the heart of the ghetto, that when he was growing up, "It wasn't nice but it was blackness. It's black now but the unity's gone." Curtis remembers that when he was a boy in the ghetto, the family could go downtown and leave their doors unlocked. "At that time, this town was decent," he says. "The morals were intact."

"Friends ain't like the way they used to be," Lonnie says. "So-called friends, they stab you in the back." "I had a lot of good friends in my neighborhood," Gordon says. "Friendship was like real friendship then. Not like friendship today." Pete remembers his school in Harlem. "Back then, the teachers really wanted the kids to learn. They took a pride in that. Now we've got a lot of kids coming out that don't even know how to read.

They're just being pushed through." Simone tells of a mother who abandoned her when she was a baby and an alcoholic father who beat her regularly. Yet she says, "It was nice at home. I grew up in a nice family. There was no abuse, nothing like that."

One striking feature about our guests is that they rarely go home again. "I have a brother in New York but I don't know where," James says. Some are reluctant to go back because they cannot get along with their relatives. Curtis' siblings turned their backs on him when he became destitute. Others cannot go home again because there is no home — their families are scattered or in overcrowded quarters and unable or unwilling to take them in. Some are simply ashamed to go back. Gordon is ashamed to go home, even to visit, unless he is in good shape with good clothes on his back and good money in his pocket — which is rarely the case.

This is true of some of our white, middle-class guests as well. Eric, the industrial engineer, never sees any members of his family. "I have a sister I never see, two brothers I never see and a twenty-year-old daughter I never see, plus three ex-wives I never see." Walter's well-to-do brother moved away and never sent his address. Kenneth, desperately sick and homeless, went to visit his affluent brother who made it clear that he did not want Kenneth around. Sidney, elderly and depressed, has a successful brother who never visits him, never phones, and has never given Sidney his address or phone number. He simply sends a check once a month which pays for Sidney's room and bus fare to and from the soup kitchens — with nothing left over. But most middle-class unemployed can go home, if necessary. They are more fortunate — and less conspicuous. Only a few show up in the soup kitchens, though their number is increasing.

The homeless mentioned here include a prostitute, a dedicated Muslim, ex-convicts, drug-addicts, alcoholics, veterans and skilled and unskilled workmen. They represent a variety of skills: a railroad man, carpenters, electricians, an artist, a heavy machinery operator, a classical pianist, a welder, construction workers, a furrier, an industrial engineer, a chef and a professional soldier. Almost all can turn their hands to many different jobs — and have — but feel a sense of betrayal that they are now not able to use any of their skills. As Morgan says, "It's unfortunate that I have to be unemployed." And Hughie, in a poignant comment on homelessness, says, "It's hard having no place to rest or take care of your hygiene. It's hard." Homelessness is not only painful, a denial of basic physical needs, it is also, in a society that considers poverty a crime, shameful.

Many of these people have been brought up, to a greater or lesser degree, as Christians (except for one very devout Black Muslim) and look to God rather than government for redress of grievances. The threat of severe cuts in Welfare, however, galvanized many into action and they formed their own organization. In this, the shelters and the soup kitchens, by bringing the homeless together, played a significant and unexpected role.

THE KITCHEN*

The people in the soup kitchen have no teeth. They cannot bite the hand that feeds them. They simply stand and wait. They are used to waiting, just as they are used to having things disappear: their jobs, their homes, their families, their Welfare checks, their luck — and their teeth.

They wait outside, and inside they wait again in a line that extends around the room, through the hall and out the door. Some laugh and joke as they wait, some come in alone and stand in silence with their hands in their pockets as if afraid of losing them, too. Their clothes scarcely change with the weather. Even in winter, most guests (men, women and children) wear the standard garb of the soup kitchen: T-shirts, jeans and jackets, which is also the standard dress of the society at large, outside of the office and the Board Room, as if the entire population were of the same age and class and sex. At a time when the rich are getting richer and the poor

* Everything described here actually happened but not all on the same evening.

poorer, the superficial trappings of equality have increased in clothes and speech and culture.

But in the soup kitchen, the jeans are faded and sometimes torn (due to wear not fashion) and the jackets are short and thin. There are hats of all kinds: stocking caps, cowboy hats, hoods, fedoras, African and Muslim hats, head scarves and a variety of caps, their peaks up or down. Earlier, all caps were worn backwards but when the Whites in town copied this style, most of the peaks in the soup kitchen moved around to the front again. Every article is clearly marked with something: brand names, firm names, team name, place names, insignia, logos. Everyone is a walking advertisement. The clothes are often colorful — red, blue, green, orange — though the more neatly dressed seem to prefer black. There are occasional earrings, sunglasses and headphones. People keep their outdoor clothes on and most keep their belongings with them at all times, even sleeping bags and backpacks.

Two students from the Carlyle School of Nursing are usually in attendance every night and, once a week, students from the Carlyle Law School provide free legal services. But no dentist ever comes to the soup kitchen.[1]

Here the homeless and the hungry can, for a little while, sit down in warmth, comfort and companionship and use the restrooms, for there are no public facilities in town, except in the railway station, which is a considerable distance away, and the library which is closed much of the time because of the city's huge budget deficit. Here the homeless are guests and, like guests, they are served. The serving table divides us: the volunteers almost entirely white, on one side, and the guests, largely

[1] The Community Health Clinic in the ghetto offers dental aid to the poor but there are long waits for treatment. I tried to interest my dentist in persuading his colleagues to establish a free dental clinic and to volunteer their services. This has been done in at least one other city. But it has not been done here.

African Americans, on the other. But here the usual roles are reversed. Here it is the privileged who cook and clean and serve and the deprived who are the guests. Yet they are guests only in the sense that they do not pay. But neither do they have any rights. They must accept what is offered.

"Guests!" Luther says scornfully. "Sounds like I drove up in a limousine, don't it?" He wears a fez and a long, loose, multi-colored jacket and carries a fat book with the title, *Sociology,* on the spine. I am waiting to take the count and he stares at my clipboard and pencil. "You know what you are?" he says. "You're a cryptologist, that's what you are."

"No," Malcolm, an elderly white man with a cane, says. "She's a count-ess."

"Welcome to the Monday night soup kitchen," Harper says, and recites the menu for the evening and the individuals or group that prepared it. This is followed by several announcements: "Save your cups for seconds. They're expensive and we want to spend our money on food not paper. Please clean off your tables before leaving. The Recreation Center will be open this Wednesday as usual. If you have any ideas for programs, bring them along. I need your input. There will be no soup kitchen on New Year's Eve. Clothes to be given away are on the tables at the back of the room. A woman's jacket, belonging to one of the volunteers, has been stolen. Will whoever took it, please return it to the CCSK office. It's not right that a volunteer who gives of her time and energy, should be repaid in this way."

The jacket was returned. But by then, the volunteer had received a brand new one, free, from L. L. Bean. She was tired of the old one anyway.

The fear of theft is, intermittently, of concern to the volunteers. Occasionally a handbag has been stolen, including mine, and my tape recorder disappeared one evening when I was working late. Most volunteers take this in stride. Actually, thefts are rare which, under the circumstances,

I find surprising. Sylvia, my least favorite volunteer, disagrees. "Poverty," she says firmly, "is no excuse for stealing."

"Maureen is in the hospital with a broken leg," Harper announces. He circulates some get-well cards and everyone signs. "Today is Ray's birthday." Applause and loud cheers. "Sam just found a job." Applause and cheers again. Al, the Green Beret veteran, makes a passionate speech, as he does every night, warning of the proposed cuts in Welfare and urging people to attend rallies and marches. The proposals are drastic. Among the most important to our guests are:

> Abolish GA (General Assistance, also called City Welfare) for all able-bodied persons, including drug addicts. This would mean not only the loss of Welfare checks for people who have no other means of support, but of rent subsidies, Medicaid, heat, and food stamps as well.
>
> Close two of the city's shelters, which were already grossly inadequate, leaving only one and a few private shelters; not nearly enough to take care of the homeless. Qualifications for admission to the city shelter will be the same as for GA.
>
> Reduce the amount paid to AFDC (Aid to Families with Dependent Children) and their rent subsidies. This is for single parent families only, which actually helps to create single parent families. Also, women who give birth while on Welfare will no longer receive child support.
>
> Reduce unemployment insurance payment from twenty-six weeks to twenty.

Cut the funds for substance abuse treatments.

Deny GA for three months to anyone who missed Workfare, even for a perfectly legitimate reason.

Moved by the threat of these cuts, many from our kitchen joined the marches and rallies. Along with other homeless people from around the city, they formed their own organization, PEOPLE FIRST, under the dedicated leadership of Joshua, a graduate of Carlyle. As a student, he helped to open the Jewish students' Kosher Kitchen to the homeless every Sunday when the churches were closed and now works tirelessly — with virtually no salary — for Help for the Homeless, concentrating on the kitchens of the CCSK.

Some of our guests are especially enthusiastic members of PEOPLE FIRST. Ray, who learned tattooing in prison, designed leaflets, political posters, banners and T-shirts which are sometimes clever, sometimes gruesome but always eye-catching. Others circulated petitions and leaflets, some wrote letters to the newspapers. PEOPLE FIRST has carried out voter registration drives and demonstrations both in New Hope and in the state capital. A small group went to see the mayor, others spoke at meetings of local businessmen and landlords, and several testified more than once at state legislative hearings.

Kate, Brian, Ted and I often went to their rallies and marches and walked with the protestors, behind signs that read: "WORK NOT WELFARE" accompanied by shouts reminiscent of the anti-Vietnam marches.

"What do we want?"

"JOBS!"

"When do we want them?"

"NOW!"

Once I joined a demonstration at the state capital. The bus ride there and back was loud with songs and laughter and general exuberance, as if the very ability to act with others as part of a movement was exhilarating. Joshua passed out free cigarettes and everyone smoked, including me, though I gave up smoking long ago.

On the bus I found myself sitting beside Julian, a young white man with a mournful expression, as if ready and waiting for the next catastrophe. I had seen him at the soup kitchen once or twice, always alone and aloof. He seemed to live inside a circle of silence, and silent people make me uneasy. He was holding a battered suitcase on his lap. "Planning to spend the night in the Governor's mansion?" I asked.

He grinned and patted the case. "This wouldn't be much use if I did. It's not really a suitcase at all. It's a traveling library." He opened it and I saw that it was filled with books, the lid arranged like a filing cabinet, holding papers and pamphlets. "Guess I got used to reading when I was studying to be a Catholic priest," he says shyly, "but I got interested in philosophy instead. And now I'm a devout pagan, though I can still quote the Bible." He sleeps in Green Wood Park, in a quiet spot he found among a clump of trees behind the University Music School and stows his sleeping bag and backpack there. "Right now I'm reading *The Comparative Method — Beyond Qualitative and Quantitative Strategies.* And I've just discovered that that's the method I've been using all along," he said with delight.

"Are you writing philosophy as well as reading it?"

"Oh, yes. I do my writing in the University library. It's pretty quiet there and I can even use their books, long as I don't take them out. No one seems to bother about me. I should be there right now but thought I'd better come along and give PEOPLE FIRST some moral support." He smiled. And then I noticed his eyelids begin to droop. It was probably the first chance he'd had to sleep in a warm, comfortable place. We had reached the capital—but I let him sleep. I did not see him again until much later, though I kept watching for him.

Could *I* have dozed off on the bus and dreamed that amazing conversation?

We demonstrated in front of the State House with speeches by Joshua and Ray and Ralph and then marched around the building. I walked beside Jack, a very thin young man who had lost an arm in a landmine in Vietnam.

"Serves me damn right for being there," he said. "I thought the Vietnamese really wanted us over there, to keep their country from being taken over by the Communists. But when we sailed into Cameron Bay, I saw Esso tankers and Texaco tankers. That meant there was a lot of American money at stake there and I saw what the war was really all about. After we got there, everybody, I think, had some kind of awakening, unless they were sociopaths and just wanted to kill. It was an American landmine that got my arm. I was lucky. I'll never forget what those mines did to the Vietnamese—old people, women, kids even. I've got my missing arm to remind me."

And to remind me, I thought, of how the country was treating its veterans. Through him, I learned that even the soldiers in Vietnam had no illusions about the war they were forced to fight.

Members of PEOPLE FIRST also camped out in tents in the cold and the rain on the New Hope Green to demonstrate what would happen if the cuts went through. "Except homeless people don't have tents," Josie pointed out.

PEOPLE FIRST held regular weekly meetings and was hard at work setting up a Day Center. Suddenly, this amorphous collection of individuals, faceless, voiceless and utterly powerless, has become a solid group with a strong identity, a voice and the potential of exerting political influence.

To the members of PEOPLE FIRST, it was an exhilarating experience which often spilled over into the atmosphere of the soup kitchen.

After the announcements, Harper asks for a guest to "bless the food," and I am reminded that I am in a church. Charlene, a small, raucous, young African American, steps forward and sternly commands the men to remove their hats and all of us to bow our heads. "Bless this food," she commands the Lord, "and bless the people who cooked it and the people who serve it." (And the people who eat it, I think.) Charlene finishes, the crowd dutifully says "Amen," Harper shouts, "Let's eat!" and, at last, the line begins to move.

The food varies a good deal. Soup — when thicker, it is called stew — consists largely of vegetables with some pieces of meat thrown in, usually chicken, and served in Styrofoam cups. It is evidently very filling and the guests seem to like it. They rarely complain about the food, at least not to us, except for dietary reasons. One night, when the main dish was pork and beans, several guests, who were new to me, announced angrily that they were Muslims and could not eat it. There is also bread or bagels with peanut butter and jelly, and muffins and doughnuts or coffee cake. For drinks, there is tea, coffee, Kool Aid and hot chocolate. The milk for the coffee is usually powdered and there is sugared water, for the sugar tends to disappear. Sometimes we serve chili or franks and beans, or pasta or canned hash, eaten off paper plates. Sometimes there is salad or fruit, usually canned. Food donated by the University dining halls is very good with a variety of dishes including solid meat (rare and much appreciated), fish, vegetables, salads, fancy cakes, even ice cream. Sometimes the remains from parties are donated: platters of canapés, cold cuts, salad and pastries — but rarely enough to go around. Once in a great while, there are candy bars, considered a great treat.

But the main fare, on two evenings at least, is likely to be soup and bread with peanut butter and jelly, filled out with doughnuts or muffins or coffee cake. Many of the guests are filling out as well.

There is a constant fear that we will run out of food before everyone has been served at least once. We never know how many guests to expect which makes planning extremely difficult. The numbers are usually somewhere over a hundred — sometimes fewer but often many more. Attendance depends on the weather, the arrival of Welfare checks and food stamps, changes in the living arrangements of our guests, or other causes which remain mysterious.

"Good evening," I say, as the guests move past me. "How are you tonight, Seth (or Ralph or Samantha)?" "Howyadoin?" some say in return; or "Can't complain," or "Hangin in there," or "Good," or simply, "Yourself?" After a while, a few even say "Good evening."

"Hereyago," the volunteers say, handing out dripping cups of soup and slices of bread. The guests pour the salt, pepper and Hot Sauce vigorously, providing their own savor. Napkins and small packets of salt are handed out by a volunteer to prevent them from disappearing.

"Any onions in that soup?" a young man asks. "Onions make me sick." But there are always onions in the soup. "That soup have meat?" someone else says. "I don't eat no meat." "This is a soup kitchen not a restaurant," Sylvia says.

"Don't be playin politics with the food, man," Conrad says and grins. "An don't be givin me no sloppy cup." "You got any soft bread?" Moses says, pointing to the slices of hard Italian bread. "I can't chew that." He smiles, showing a completely empty mouth. "What we got here, doll?" Amos says, staring into the enormous pot. "Holocaust stew? I can't eat that stuff. President Reagan wouldn't eat that stuff. You wouldn't eat that stuff.

Punish the poor, that's what it is. Humiliate and incarcerate and disenfranchise the poor." But he laughs loudly and comes back for seconds.

Some of the guests are silent as they go down the line. They wear dark glasses and headphones and their caps pulled down low, as if to protect themselves from a prying and hostile world. A few seem resentful or embarrassed, some are shy, some boisterous, some jokingly flirtatious. There are compliments, invitations to dinner, "You married? Your husband jealous?" Sometimes the give and take is reversed and gifts come from the other side of the table: Christmas cards, Valentine cards, a flower, a plant, a tiny bottle of Vidal Sassoon's hair lotion, poems, even a basket of delicacies, brought to my house at Christmas time by Morgan who lives nearby.

Alex says that since he stopped drinking, he is always hungry. Troy, an extremely thin, dark-haired young man, wants extra salad for the rabbits in the local cemetery. Last night, I drove him and his wife there and waited while they stood in the freezing cold with their short jackets and gloveless hands, patiently tossing bits of lettuce over the high fence. But tonight there is no salad. Frank, a carpenter, who was full of excitement when he won a scholarship to a woodcarving class, brings in a sample of his work. My husband and I commission a plaque.

Jerry, a lively, young blond in ragged jeans, a ponytail, a single earring and a cross around his neck, arrives carrying a suit on a hanger. He wants permission to hang it in the soup kitchen overnight as he needs it for court tomorrow. The homeless, I suddenly realize, have nowhere to keep their clothes except stuffed into shopping bags. I ask if he would like a friend in court and he responds with thanks. Kate and I agree to go.

"We'll start with *Coquille St. Jacques,*" I hear someone on the line say, "and go on to *boeuf en brochette.*" It is Eric who is usually silent as he waits on line, except for an occasional comment to the server about the seasoning in the soup. Yet last month he sold me tickets to the New Hope Chorale in which he sings and earlier showed me a portfolio of his photographs: dramatic, black and white promo pictures of actors and dancers, offered to them free. Last week he handed me an announcement of a one-man show of his paintings. A few of us from the soup kitchen went to the opening and one of Eric's paintings now hangs in my study.

Sidney is white, elderly and well-dressed in a wide-brimmed, tan hat and a tan overcoat. He has been in and out of mental hospitals and walks with his head down and a dejected expression. "How are you tonight, Sidney?" I ask. He looks up and smiles. "I am enjoying life to the fullest," he says as he reaches for his soup. Last week, Kenneth, a tall, aloof white man who, for many nights, barely responded to my greeting, handed me his dossier. He is a classical concert pianist and teacher. Tonight he tells me that he will be accompanying a singer in a concert next month. I congratulate him and tell him I'd like to come.

The handsome African American woman is always alone, speaks to no one, answers no one and always looks angry. She seems to be wearing all her clothes at once. They hang down, one beneath the other, under a bulky red jacket, creating that "layered look," dictated, in this case, not by fashion but necessity. Her head is completely covered with a red cloth which she never removes. She carries her belongings with her in several heavy bags and, it is said, sleeps on a window ledge of the public library. Most nights, she merely glances at the food and walks on, taking nothing but bread and coffee which she eats alone at the back of the room.

She was once a high school teacher, I was told, from a middle-class family. But she had a bad experience with a man — jilted? raped? — took to drink, or was it drugs? — and was rejected by her family. Though no one knows her name, I think of her as Dido, handsome, majestic — and abandoned. She has occasional loud, sudden outbursts in good English and excellent diction. "I have no place to sleep," she shouts. "No place where my children, my family can visit me. But no one cares." She stamps out without waiting for an answer.

Tonight she peers into the enormous soup pot and says: "I can't eat that. I'm diabetic. Don't you have any other soup kitchen for people who can't eat this food? Or at least give out money or food vouchers to people with eating disorders. So we can buy some decent food."

"We can't start catering to special needs," Sylvia says. But Dido stalks off without waiting for an answer, as if she already knew what it would be. She never came back.

"What did you read today, Walter?" I ask, as I do every night. "I've just finished *Le Philosophe sans le Savoir* by Sedaine, who wrote eighteenth century comedies," he said, "and I've decided to go back to Tacitus as my Latin is becoming quite rusty." He is more formally dressed than most for he wears a tie and jacket over his jeans and a topcoat. He might be a pharmacist or an accountant out to lunch. He speaks rapidly in clear, correct English with precise diction. I knew nothing about him until he asked me one night if I had ever read Dostoevski's *Notebooks for Crime and Punishment.* After that, we managed to discuss books quite often.

Stu, a tall, thin African American is very restless. He prowls around the room constantly. Sometimes he is friendly, even amusing, and we have had a good joking relationship ever since we discovered that our birthdays fall on the same date. But sometimes he seems tense and wild-eyed, breaking into the line many times. When accused, he jokes, "Not me, man. That was my twin brother. I got lotsa twin brothers," or he reacts with fierce anger.

"Stoned," one of the volunteers whispers. We are reluctant to challenge him and the other guests laugh, shrug and let him get ahead of them in the line. No one wants any trouble.

Last night, when he came through the line for the fourth time, I looked at Kate and nodded significantly in his direction. He saw me and became furious. "You got somethin to say bout me, you say it to my face!" he shouted. "I got somethin to say bout you, I'll say it to *your* face." He wants to be treated with respect. I agreed that he should be. I apologized. I tried to shake hands but he kept on shouting. I kept on apologizing. Finally, Brian called out, "Hey, Helen, are there any more doughnuts?" effectively interrupting the scene. Stu walked away, grabbing the last remaining doughnut as he went.

"Thanks," I told Brian. "Sure you're not a psychologist?" He grinned. "No, still just a lawyer." Tonight I try again to make my peace with Stu. After a good deal of apologizing on my part, he relents. We shake hands. But we both know that I will never interfere with him again. Peace at any price. Besides, I tell myself, he is tall and very thin. Perhaps he needs all that extra food.

We have a new volunteer tonight, a visitor named Colin. He is tall and blonde with a pleasant smile and a British accent. Stu, coming through the line for the third time, suddenly notices him. "You new here, aincha?" he says. I introduce them and add that Colin is a visitor to the US.

"Yeah? Where from?" Stu says.

"South Africa."

I can see Stu winding up for action. "You a racist?" he says.

"I wouldn't be here if I were, would I?" Colin says calmly. He holds out his hand and, after a brief pause, Stu takes it and they shake in a special way. "That's the way we shake in South Africa," Colin says. "But you do something different here."

"Yeah," Stu says, "like this." He demonstrates and they smile and shake hands again.

Spike, a rather short but muscular African American with a huge smile and a boisterous manner, laughs and jokes his way down the line. He was badly injured in a construction accident several years ago and has not worked since. At the moment, he is homeless. He comes to the soup kitchen early and leaves late, and sometime falls asleep during dinner. But he always works, setting up tables and chairs before dinner, scrubbing the pots and pans afterward. "Yeah, I learned how to wash dishes," he says when I compliment him on the good job he is doing. "I had to. That's the only way I could be sure of eatin."

He recently left his rooming house because of the crime and the drugs and the violence. "How'm I gonna find another place when I got no car and no phone and no money for pay phones or bus fare?" When I ask about his family, he says, "My family don't communicate. Know how I spent Christmas? Sittin in that smelly room all alone. Starin at the stars." I made an appointment for him with the social worker at Jefferson House, the best and largest shelter in town, and drove him to the interview. But, in the end, he refused to get out of the car. "No," he said. "No shelter. They always make trouble for me in the shelter. An, see, I'm tryin to stay outta trouble."

I allowed him to use my phone number for calls about apartments and gave him money for a motel room on one of the coldest nights. We spent hours driving around, inspecting possible rentals. But the nicer places were too expensive and the cheaper ones were in bad neighborhoods which he would not even consider. "I gotta be very choicy," he kept saying. "Because, see, they're out to get me." I regarded this as sheer paranoia. But tonight, two strange men walked into the soup kitchen with guns tucked under their jackets. They were looking for Spike. For the first time in weeks, Spike wasn't there.

A man in filthy jeans with filthy hands who clearly lives on the street, shuffles in late. He keeps his head down, speaks to no one and no one speaks to him — except when he reaches for a doughnut. “Don’t touch the food,” Sylvia shouts, jumping forward and waving him away. A plastic hand extends a doughnut. He takes it and walks on, his head bent lower than ever. Though he has been coming to the soup kitchen for weeks, I have never seen his face. “They can at least be clean,” Sylvia says. “It doesn’t cost anything to be clean.”

“Don’t talk to me. I’m in a bad mood,” Cliffie shouts from the doorway. He is a short, stocky African American in a tight, black jacket, stiff as a breastplate and zipped to the chin. He wears a purple stocking hat bound up in a scarf and looks like a child with mumps. He never, during the evening, unzips his jacket or unties his scarf or takes off his hat. No one sees his hair from November to May. His face is still young but his body has grown stout, thanks to a steady diet of bread, soup and alcohol. “I’m starting a detox program next week,” he announces periodically. But he never does.

He was a student some years ago in a literacy class where I worked as a volunteer. On my first night in the soup kitchen, he spotted me from across the room and shouted, “Hey, don’t I know you? Sure I do. I know you. You’re my teacher.” He rushed up, threw an arm around me and went on shouting to the kitchen at large, “Know what? She was my teacher. Up to the Community Center. Yeah. Ain’t that sumpin?” This, he seems to feel, gives him a claim on me, in spite of the fact that I never managed to teach him anything.

“I’m not eatin tonight. I don’t feel good,” he says now. But he stares into the soup anyway. “Don’t give me none of that fat,” he commands. “An I don’t want no carrots. I want meat.” He goes on staring into the pot, taking his time, looking for the biggest piece of meat in the virtually meatless vegetable soup, while behind him the queue grows impatient.

"C'mon, Cliffie. Move it! You're holdin up the line."

But Cliffie was not to be rushed. "There, that piece, there," he says pointing, with his finger almost in the soup. "An that one, too. That big one. But no juice. I don't want no juice. I'm in a bad mood," he repeats. "That social worker won't give me my check till Monday. How'm I gonna make it through the weekend?" He "borrows" $3.00 from Nan after promising not to spend it on drink. Then he settles down, as always, with the young student nurses to have his blood pressure checked, to talk about his ailments, and to wait for me, as always, to give him a ride to a neighborhood bar or convenience store. He will stay there until the bars and restaurants close at around 2:00 AM. Then he will start his round of collecting bottles and cans from the trash bins outside.

He lives in a rooming house inhabited entirely by Welfare recipients, many of whom come to the soup kitchen, and he enjoys gossiping about them to the volunteers. "Tucker's back from jail and boozin and druggin again," he tells us. "Doreen had two abortions already this year. Deirdre's boyfriend threw her out so she's livin on the street again."

"Lemme aks you a question," he booms at me again. "You givin me a ride tonight?" But it is not really a question. It's a command. I have been giving him a ride just about every night so that it has become, not a gift, but a right. It's useless to tell him I won't be leaving for a long time. "I'll wait," he says and sits down, tightly packed and round as a doorknob with his huge containers of "take-outs" and his bag for bottles and cans beside him. He waits patiently and watches while we clean up but he never helps, even when I suggest it. He simply sits and waits, shouting periodically, "Hey, Helen. Lemme aks you a question. You gonna take me home tonight, aincha?" Finally the other volunteers shout back, "For God's sake,

Helen, take him home. Do us a favor and get him out of here."

Difficult as he is, we all indulge him. Perhaps because he is so colorful and so childlike; or perhaps we sense that, cheated as he has been by both nature and nurture, he continues to fight back in the only way he knows.

In spite of the rule against "lending" money to the guests, we are sometimes, though rarely, approached. Woody wants to buy Pampers for his new baby. Laurie, a youngish white woman, needs money for sanitary napkins. Frederick needs train fare to Stanton to visit his girl in the hospital. Occasionally, there is an emergency: Jackson and his girlfriend are about to be evicted and need rent money. Pete wants money for a license to drive a bus. There's a job waiting. Considering the grotesque economic discrepancy between guests and hosts, it is a rule some find hard to obey. And often don't.

Muriel lives on the street, has a paralyzed arm and lugs several heavy bags around with her. The other guests avoid her as much as possible for she smells. She is a thin white woman with curly dark hair and is quite attractive — until she smiles. She is getting thinner and thinner, losing more and more teeth, becoming more and more hostile, and laughs and shouts in an irrational manner. Increasingly angry and paranoid, she complains constantly of being "hassled" by the guests and insulted by the volunteers. Last night she was louder and more out of control than usual. When she deliberately spilled her coffee all over Charlene, she was removed and served outside. The fact that her boyfriend, who also lived on the street, was murdered as he lay sleeping beside her, has probably not improved her mental state. Her attitude toward me, though we have had fairly long talks, especially at the Rec Center, has become unpredictable and her speech incoherent. Tonight she smiles and hands me a paper bag. It contains four rotting bananas. A misguided gift? Or an insult wrapped in a metaphor? I smile back and thank her.

Marshall, a young African American with a gentle face and a soft voice, is covered with bruises and cuts. He does not eat but sits down at an empty table with his head in his hands. When I ask what happened, he begins to cry. He was mugged in the Y again and had his Welfare check stolen. "My doctor says I should get out of there," he says. "But where can I go?"

Some guests help themselves to extra packets of salt and pepper and quantities of paper napkins. For a while, they even took the toilet paper. The churches complained, the bathrooms were locked, and Harper walked around with the keys in his pocket and a roll of tissue under his arm. Tonight, one of the guests asks me, in a whisper, for paper napkins to take home to use for toilet paper.

Lloyd, a tall, neat, well-spoken African American, asks to borrow my pencil. He returns a short time later with a poem, neatly written on a paper napkin and I offer to type it for him. He writes one almost every night now about the soup kitchen and about people and incidents in the ghetto. They are surprisingly good. Gary has written a letter to the newspaper about the homeless and wants me to correct and type it. Later, he brings poems, too, as do several others, for me to type. Samantha, a big, handsome, noisy African American, surprised me one night with a moving poem about her dead son. She wrote several more on other nights and read one of them at the Wednesday night Cabaret. Deirdre, whose speech is often slurred and incoherent, wrote a long, grateful poem to the volunteers which she read one evening before grace.

Magda is a small, elderly white woman with a well-poised hat and a genteel manner. She is a great favorite with the volunteers and gets along extremely well with the guests. She usually comes rather late and, instead of taking her place at the end of the line, marches straight up to the front. Everyone, guests and volunteers alike, pretend they have not seen this.

During dinner, she talks earnestly with the guests near her. "Spike is ill," she tells me later with a slight foreign accent (German, Scandinavian, Dutch?). "Such a nice man. But, of course, he is ill. With no home, how could he not be ill? Could you maybe give him a job here? He works so hard. Maybe you could pay him something for all that work, yes?" I tell her I am only a volunteer but that I will ask Harper. She remains something of a mystery. Though extremely friendly, she refuses to reveal anything about herself, not even where she is from. I see her often in the library, reading a Japanese newspaper.

At about 6:30, if everyone has been served once, Harper announces "Seconds" which some prefer to take home. " Take-outs" are carried out in the bright, blue, plastic wrappers of *The New York Times* brought in by the volunteers. These are conspicuous all over town providing free advertisements for *The Times,* courtesy of the homeless.

Adrian hurries in looking, as always, as if he'd been blown in. His jacket is unbuttoned and his hair stands on end. He is scantily dressed, as always, even in winter, and without hat or gloves. He is white, young, thin and eats very little. Product of an upper-class family and an upper-class private school, he hangs around the serving table, talking to the volunteers long after the other guests have gone. He wonders where he can find Utopia. He went to Disney World, thinking it might be there, but it was disappointing. "The buildings were ugly and the rides silly," he says. He comes to the soup kitchen regularly except on holidays when he goes home to his family. At the end of winter, he always disappears for a longer period. "I went to the hospital," he explains when he returns. "I always get depressed in the spring." He reads a good deal and likes to browse in The Good Samaritan, a Christian bookshop. "Right now I'm reading Gothic romances," he says. "Hawthorne and Hardy: *The Scarlet Letter* and *Jude, the Obscure. Jane*

Eyre, too. I like the nineteenth century. All that language."

Ray and Ralph arrive late, suited and tied and brushed and scrubbed and are hailed by the guests. They have just come back from the state capital where they spent the night in Tent City in front of the State House and testified at a committee meeting. They wore their PEOPLE FIRST T-shirts under their jackets, Ralph reports with delight, and flashed them at the committee before speaking. Much laughter and applause from the guests. The governor refused to see them. "I stuck a leaflet on his car," Ralph says. More laughter and cheers. Joshua rushed up to him as he was leaving and invited him to come to Tent City and have a cup of soup. But he refused. He said that "with the bad economy, everybody in the state has to bite the bullet, rich and poor alike." There is a loud moan and then silence to the sound, I imagine, of gnashing teeth.

Reg arrives just before closing time, as usual, not rushing in like the others, but sauntering slowly, pompously, making an entrance like an African prince in a long, loose, multi-colored shirt and matching hat, with carved African figures hanging from his neck. His speech is careful, deliberate, with no trace of a southern accent. He eats alone, surrounded by admiring females and extra portions of food which he always manages to acquire. When he leaves, he takes bags of food with him.

Last night, Lewis, a volunteer and coordinator of the Tuesday night soup kitchen, saw him bending over the water cooler near the kitchen.

"Sorry, sir," Lewis said, "but we're supposed to use the one in the back."

Reg's poise disappeared. Even his speech changed. "That's got hairs floatin on top. I'm sure not drinkin outta that."

"Sorry, but I can't let you use this one. Orders from the church."

"Listen, man," Reg said, "no one's tellin me what I can and can't do. I'm drinkin from this here cooler and there ain't nothin you can do about it."

"Oh, yes there is! I can have the police down here before you have a chance to swallow."

"Oh, no you won't. You git outta my face before I knock you down. You hear me, man? I said, git outta my face."

It seemed that violence was about to erupt. Instead, Reg went storming out with Lewis at his heels. "He's okay," Lewis said when he came back. "A nice guy, really."

Tonight, Reg arrives looking calm, cool and poised as always.

There have been very few disturbances in the kitchen. Those that did occur were brief and nothing Harper couldn't handle. He has never called the police. Tonight there are loud shouts from the back of the room where Spike, good-natured but short-tempered, is getting ready for a punch-out with Leander, a large man whose face looks as if it had been stepped on at birth. "Break it up," Harper says quietly. "NOW." Leander moves to another table but Spike continues to shout. "I jes sittin here, eatin my dinner an tryin to keep outta trouble. But that man givin me so much grief." He starts toward Leander's table but Harper puts an arm around him and walks him to the door. "Go on out and cool off," he says. "Then you can come back in."

The ambulance has come twice: once for a pregnant woman and once for the guest with dirty hands who collapsed mysteriously but quietly beside the bread table. We saw his face for the first time.

A small, dark man, in a huge overcoat who smiles but never talks, is picking food out of the large garbage can near the door.

"Yes, I'm working," Paul says, a white man with long hair, thick glasses and a frightened expression that seems to have settled down permanently between brow and chin. "Sweeping under the viaduct for 50¢ an hour." His teeth are rotting and he needs a haircut but can't afford it. "I can't look for a decent job like this," he says. The clinic promised him new teeth two years ago. But will he find a job even with a haircut and a new set of teeth?

For many, the soup kitchen is a welcome relief from loneliness and boredom as well as hunger. "In the beginning, I felt ashamed to come," Kenneth, the classical pianist, says, "but I don't feel that way now. You can't go on being ashamed all your life."

"If you're not working, it breaks up the monotony," Hal says. "You come down at 6:00, have dinner and lose a whole hour. I watch 'Star Trek' at 7:00 and then it's 8:00 o'clock and the night's beginning to move on."

"We really get a lot, you know, at the kitchen," Leeta says. "I mean like food and clothes and blankets. Everybody treats you nice. An it's nice to just get out." "I come to the soup kitchen because it's around people," Michelle, a prostitute and drug addict, says. "It gives me a break from the drugs."

Some acquire friends here. "I found a couple of people I can share my load with," Pete, the truck driver says, though in the beginning he had a funny feeling about coming. "Getting a hand-out, looking like a bum. But as you get on, you know that all these people are in a situation similar to yours." Jonathan and Sandy met in the soup kitchen. "He's congenial," Jonathan says. "I found out he's a neighbor and we walk down here together." Ray was homeless when he met Josie. Now they share her room, an established couple. "I met Eugene in the soup kitchen last summer," Simone says, "and we're still together. Ain't that sumthin?"

A few prefer to take their food out to eat elsewhere, and some like to sit alone and eat in silence. "The soup kitchen is not a social affair to me," Tyler, a thoughtful but morose young African American, says. "I don't have any friends in the soup kitchen," Lonnie says. "I'm ashamed to come," Curtis, a dignified electrician, says, "but I have no choice. I'm glad my father can't see me."

Most, however, seem to enjoy themselves, eating and talking and laughing together, men and women, Black, White and Hispanic, young, middle-aged and old; an AIDS sufferer and a classical pianist; an ex-convict and Magda, sipping daintily. Many come in alone and go out alone but, for a little while, they are part of a group. Sometimes it's quiet, sometimes noisy with much laughter and shouting. A middle-aged African American man plays the piano softly for a long time — without using his thumbs. Another plays "The Moonlight Sonata" which he picked up by ear in the hospital. But Kenneth, the classical pianist, never touches the piano. Sometimes, children bang on it for a while, making the room uncomfortably noisy. Sometimes Harper brings a "boom box" that plays very loud rock music. It is a colorful, sociable scene, almost like a restaurant except that the diners are something more than a collection of strangers and less than a group of friends. And they are eating in their hats and coats.

The Voices

THE MOTHERS

"Rachel weeping for her children"
—*Jeremiah 31:15*

Leeta (reformed drug addict)
Josie (naïve optimist)
Michelle (prostitute)

These three women are all quite different except that they are all weeping for their lost children. They are not only mothers without children, they are women without husbands and jobs and money as well. Two are even without homes. None of them became pregnant in order to receive Welfare checks, as is so often assumed. All have had their children taken from them and all are determined to get them back.

All have had to contend with poverty and substance abuse: Josie in the form of an alcoholic husband, Michelle and Leeta with their own drug addiction. All were victimized by unscrupulous people, Michelle especially so. Josie and Michelle were both subjected to violence.

Leeta is the most fortunate and the only one who had loving parents and supportive siblings. A pleasant, gentle woman, she is also the most pliable and was at the mercy of irresponsible men and a drug-addicted neighbor. Her children, too, became victims: her daughter who was raped by her uncle and her son through the influence of a lawless neighborhood gang; the result, Leeta believes, of her negligence. Motivated by feelings of guilt and concern, she managed to rehabilitate herself. Her children, too, are on the way to recovery. Soon she will have them back.

Josie is not so fortunate. Unlike Leeta, she is a fighter but fighting has not done her much good. Her problems are overwhelming. A willing worker, she cannot find a permanent job. A warm-hearted, generous woman, she is often betrayed by the people she tries to help. Tough and courageous, she is also surprisingly naïve and often acts impulsively and imprudently. Above all, she is trapped by the conditions of her life: a drunken, feckless and often brutal husband, dire poverty and two children whom she abandoned, she believes, for their own good. Her father died young and there is no mention of brothers or sisters. Her mother has occasionally sent her checks but even when Josie was on the street, she knew she could not go home. She has no one. We watch her thrashing about, using poor judgment with painful consequences to herself. But she refuses to be defeated. Instead she is determined to "Start over, to have a nice place to live and be happy, to have my kids back and let them start over and be happy too."

Michelle is fierce — in love and in hate — which has both helped and hurt her. Her life, from the beginning, was stormy, filled by destructive people: her teachers, her grandparents, an older cousin, her lovers (all except one) and even her mother, who first abandoned her and then turned her into a drug dealer. There was no one in her life who could help her develop — in a constructive way — the admirable traits she possessed. Yet in spite of the sordid — indeed, criminal — life she has led, she is surprisingly appealing: tough, courageous, ruthlessly honest about herself, and very intelligent. Under different circumstances, her life might have been admirable. Yet her fierce desire to have her children back may help her to save herself.

LEETA

"Right now I want a full-time job.
Or get into a program or go to school.
I want to get into somethin."

She is a short, stocky African American with her hair completely covered by a scarf. She has a rather stolid, unanimated, almost sullen expression but when addressed, she becomes very friendly with a lively manner and a big smile. In spite of her troubles, she is cheerful, seems entirely without rancor and says about the people in her family, "We've always been close." We met for the first time at the Rec Center where she readily agreed to be interviewed. She is thirty-three.

I have three children — fifteen, thirteen and three — but I never been married. I tried to hide my first baby and keep it covered. But Mama knew. She said, 'Leeta, I know.' And she took me to the doctor. I was like four months pregnant. I think I was too late. I was scared. She said, 'You know, we're gonna do the best we could.' And she stuck by my side all the way through.

"The guy I was goin with was in the Service. He wasn't much help. We never really was close. My son sees him. My daughter, she has a different father but her father, he calls my son his son, too. They was real close. He would take both the kids out just like they were both his. He never lived with us. The kids always was just with me. Fathers never helped financially. Maybe you used to find somebody would stick by you, help you financially. But now seems like everybody's just out for theirselves."

Her father worked at the Finchley factory but her mother always stayed home. "Mama and Daddy was always there. Mama used to go to things at the school when they raised money. She went to PTA meetings and stuff like that. We always lived in the house together. We were like a close family. Everyone stuck together. Mama didn't always have it good even though Daddy worked. And she went to different places where they gave out free food, cheese and stuff. I never worked while I was in school. But afterward, I always worked part-time. I never worked full-time because I always had the kids.

"My parents were old. They left the same year. Mama left, then Daddy left. Mama had diabetes and Daddy had a pacemaker. Mama was really sick. She had a hospital bed in the room and we had to take care of her for a long time. She warned us that she was gonna go soon. My brother and my sister said, 'Daddy ain't gonna make it without Mama.'

Four months after she passed, Daddy passed, too."

Leeta and her brother took over the house but a year later Leeta began to take drugs. "Seems like after our parents passed, things just didn't work out. A neighbor told me, 'You wanna try it?' I said, 'OK, I'll try it.' It was Crack. She lived across the street from me and I went over there. At first I wasn't really gettin anything at all. So I tried more and more.

"Drugs was really eatin into my money. I was gettin my Welfare check and I was still livin in our house but the house wasn't seein not one dollar. My brother and my sister, they were offa me. My brother took care of the kids.

"I was across the street smokin every day. That's all I did. I mean I just lost it. It makes you feel good. Nothin bothered me. I would stay home long enough to change my clothes, whatever, and go out again. I wouldn't eat or nuthin. I tried to hide it from my kids. But my son, he was old enough that he knew about it. We was always close. He said, 'Ma, what's wrong? Somethin's wrong, Ma,' My sister knew. She helped me. We always been close. Whenever I went across the street, she said, 'Get off that shit.'"

Her sister took the children. "I felt sad when she took the kids. I wanted to get into a program but I had to wait. Finally, they sent me up to Deep Valley. I was there forty-five days. It was hard, it really was hard. I didn't like it at first but I wanted somethin. And I didn't want nobody to know. I'm not tempted to go back to drugs." And, evidently, she hasn't.

Leeta's daughter was raped at the age of eleven by her uncle. He's in a hospital now and she's in the University Psychiatric Institute. "That's a nice place up there. But being confined, she didn't like that. Plus they keep the door locked. They buzz you in and out. She didn't like that either. It was driving her crazy. But she's doing good now.

"My son, Silvester, he's fifteen and he's just as big as me. He's in Cornwall Reform School. He's been there a year. He'll be out in October."

When he was eleven or twelve, older boys began to take him joy riding. Later, they stole cars. "He wouldn't steal no old cars. Just new ones. I knew he was into it. He was comin home late. I think part of it was because I started doin drugs. I was never home. And when I left to go to the drug program, I don't think he fully understood that. It broke him up a lot.

"One night he was ridin in a car when the police were after him. They had to ram him, head on, to make him stop. He broke his shoulder, messed up his face, broke a tooth. I thought that was gonna be the end of it. It was like, boy, you coulda lost your life. He got out of the hospital and they put him in Juvenile Detention for two weeks. He was in and out of there for like twenty times before they really did somethin with him.

"He's been arrested everywhere: West Hope, East Hope, South Hope, New Hope. Even over to Fleetwood. Every time, he was ridin in a stolen car or drivin one. Every time. And they let me take him home, every time. No bail. Or they put him in Montgomery Avenue Jail for a couple of days. They have a section now where they keep the juveniles. It's not bad. It's like a little camp. They had visits an everythin.

"I was really wore out. I had really had it. I would hate to see them put my son away but — like he was getting caught at least once a week. I didn't want to see him go to some place like that place in Blattsford. Didn't want nothin like that. But I wanted him to go to a school that would help him."

Finally, they sent him to Cornwall Reform School. "You know, he likes it. It gives him encouragement. He works and he goes to school. He plays basketball. He's on the team. I can visit and he comes home on weekends. I'm glad he's there because the streets are so bad now. My neighborhood isn't too bad but I just want him to have somethin to do, somethin to get into. He's doin good now and he feels good about it. He knows what he did an everything. He's trainin to take care of the handicapped.

When he comes out, he'll be goin to high school.

"You ever see the college newspaper? This lady was writin on street crimes and she put my son in a article. He told her what he had been into and where he was at. It was real nice. He didn't mind talkin to her at all. He's like a totally different person. Me and my son is so open. He's seen me through so much."

Two of his friends were shot on Thanksgiving weekend. "One was selling drugs and the other was just along with him. They was both shot in the street by rival drug dealers. Silvester was home on leave when that happened. Didn't say nothin bout it. Just went to his room an shut the door. Wouldn't eat no Thanksgiving dinner.

"The soup kitchens, at holidays, they're always givin out stuff. We really get a lot, you know, at the kitchens. I mean like clothing and blankets and food. Everybody treats you nice. Even if you have food at home, I mean, it's nice, just to get out. The children come to the kitchen with me. They like it. My son always comes to the night kitchen when he's home. He loves it. My daughter, she loved it when she was younger. She used to come with me at night all the time. But now she wants to be a cheerleader and she says she's too busy with practicin an all that. But I think, now she's older, it's like she's ashamed to come.

"I'm not workin now. I'm on the State. But I want a job, somethin full-time. My youngest son is three years old. He'll be goin to Head Start soon. My other son will be home in October. So I got two kids in the house that's big enough to take care of things. I'm getting worried, stayin home all the time. I want a full-time job or get into a job trainin program, or go to school, or somethin. I want to get into *somethin.*"

JOSIE

"If you can't get any food, you tell yourself you're not hungry. If it's not safe to go to sleep, you tell yourself you're not sleepy."

She is a short, stocky white woman of forty-two with brown hair cut in a Dutchboy haircut which gives her a youthful appearance. She has a hearty, out-going manner and is energetic, fearless and, at times, childishly naïve. She is irrepressibly optimistic and bounces back after every catastrophe with the words, "Let's start over." Like her boyfriend, Ray, she is very active in PEOPLE FIRST and speaks out vigorously at all protest meetings, goes on all the marches and has slept out on demonstrations in all kinds of weather. The interview was held in the Rec Center storeroom while she ate her way through an enormous pile of popcorn and a huge piece of cake.

I never knew what Welfare was. I never knew what food stamps were. I first heard about Welfare in the 9th grade because there was this girl that was on it. We knew from her clothes and I guess the way she acted; like she was scared or ashamed. Everybody used to make fun of her. I said to myself, I hope I never have to be in that situation. And I hope if I ever get married and have kids, I hope, please God, that they never have to be in that situation either."

She went to work right after high school and seems to have been a conscientious worker from the start. "I worked so many jobs, I can't remember them all. In a law firm, in Safeways, in department stores selling clothes and even men's cologne. I arranged all the bottles according to size and put everything out nice and neat."

When she met her husband, Clyde, they were both out of work. "I told him, 'Why don't we look for work, try to get a nice place and start over?' So that's what we did."

They also started a family. He worked in construction and she planted bushes and trees, which she had never done before. "I planted them in straight rows, according to size, nice and neat. Just like the cologne. But Clyde was drinking. When he wasn't drinking, he was great, he was like a different person. With alcoholism, they say, it's in the blood. He took sticks and he was going to stab me with them. He took knives. He stamped on my feet with construction shoes so I couldn't walk. I had trouble with him for years because of the drinking." Finally, she took the children and went to live with her mother. After a year, he wanted her to come back, so she did. And, as she said, they started over.

She had $800 saved up and they rented a place for $400 a month. "It had everything included: utilities, furniture, pots and pans, color TV, cable, everything. It was beautiful. It was like an apartment hotel. They even had people clean the rooms for us. And they had a machine with a red button that you pressed so you could get nice and tan. I worked from Monday through Friday cleaning offices and clinics: mopping the floors, emptying the trash, cleaning the bathrooms. I liked it. And they liked me. We all felt bad when I had to leave in the summer because the rent went up to $3,000 a month."

Clyde was offered a security job there but turned it down. "'They just want you to watch the house,' I said. 'Any fool can do that.' 'And only a fool would,' he said. 'And get his head blown off.' I was mad. If he would have took it, we still would have been there. I wouldn't have been afraid. I would take it. I've worked Security."

They decided to go to New Hope. Josie didn't want to travel too far with the children and her grandfather used to live there. Also, they heard that the rents were cheaper. But they weren't and they couldn't find a place they could afford so they lived in the car. Luckily, it was summer. One night the police came by. "They told us, 'You're in the worst part of town. You'll end up getting shot. And you've got kids. You have to move on.'" They spent many nights, driving around, trying to find a place to park. Finally, they received City Assistance and learned about the soup kitchen. But they still couldn't afford to pay rent. They lived in motels on and off and, on and off, they lived in the car.

Clyde was still drinking. One night, he grabbed her and tried to push her, head first, through the windshield. Another time, when they were visiting friends from the soup kitchen, Clyde drank heavily all evening. Suddenly, he glared at her, jumped up, dragged her from the sofa and began to shove her out of the third story window. Their friends stopped him in time. "He's crazy. He'll do it when he's drunk. I don't know why. I don't know if he's done it to other women before me. The children just accept it. It's not good but he's not violent with them. Just with me."

They met the Bumbrys in the soup kitchen and went to live with them. They were two couples who lived together with their children on money from the state. "I didn't like living there because the place was dirty, the kids ran wild, fighting and throwing food around and the parents just sat there getting stoned. They were even dealing drugs. They stole my wallet and Clyde's winter jacket he just got from the soup kitchen. One night one of their children changed the TV channel that his father was watching. The father grabbed him and beat him with a belt. They kept a belt handy on top of the TV and used it all the time.

"In the town of Morton, where I grew up, if you hit a kid with a belt, you automatically get arrested, handcuffed and sent to jail. I called DYCS (Department of Youth and Child Services) and said, 'If somebody's hitting their kids with a belt, can they get arrested?' They said, 'It depends and besides, you have to have solid proof.' I said, 'I've got solid proof. I've seen it. And besides, they've got cuts and bruises and everything else.' I got mad. 'You people don't check, you don't do anything. I don't think it's right.'

"I told my husband, 'I can't live like this. Because if these people ever get harassed in court for hitting their children and stuff, and we're living in the same house, we could get in trouble, too. I'm leaving.' And I told those Bumbrys, 'If I ever find out you're hurting my kids, believe me, I'll report you.'

"I had to leave my husband and the children. I had no choice. If I didn't, my husband would never get on AFDC (Aid For Dependent Children) because only one parent can get it. And if I got on, he'd hassle me about it. So, whether they realized it or not, the state helped to break us up. So I left and let him have the kids and he got AFDC. The thing that really gets me mad is that I could have had him arrested for trying to push me through the windshield and trying to shove me out the window. Then I could have had the kids, just like that. But I didn't. I thought, well, when my kids get older, they'll understand."

Her situation was horrendous. She had no place to go. She was homeless. "It was really degrading. I stayed in the streets in the summer, winter, whatever. I did it. I had to. Some places, I was outside, some places I was inside. Nobody would ever believe it, the places I went. It was horrible. I could never do it again."

She hated the shelter. She couldn't stand the lack of freedom and she couldn't stand the conditions. "Maybe it's different now, but back then it was terrible." One night, she felt something strange in her bed. She took a knife and cut her mattress and saw big bugs coming out of it. The staff was angry when she told them, "I've got to go. I can't live like this. I'll live in the street. I'll take a chance.

"Living in the street — it's like hell." She had no money at all. She ate in soup kitchens but she couldn't buy clothes or a toothbrush or even soap. "You take a chance where you sleep. Certain places, if you get caught, you go to jail.

"I didn't know any other homeless people then and I didn't know New Hope. I slept in the train station once or twice. You're nuts to even go in the train station at night. It's right across from the Project. I didn't know they had drugs and everything else in that Project. You'll wind up getting stabbed, killed. But all that happened was that the police threw me out. That's why I definitely believe in God."

She even slept on a bench on the Green. Several times, she heard cars pull up beside her. "You wanna come to my house? You'll be real comfortable at my house." One night, when she was fast asleep, she felt someone's breath on her face. A strange man was leaning way over her, almost on top of her. "You need a place to stay, sweetheart?" he said softly. "I've got a nice place. A real nice place." She struggled up, gave him a solid push and ran. "God certainly helped me that night. I had plenty of opportunities to sleep indoors, in a real bed. But I never took the chance. I wasn't molested. I wasn't attacked. Because I knew how to take care of myself. I'd just tell them right out, 'Leave me alone or you'll go to jail.' Most guys just back off and say, 'Forget it.'" Or was she just lucky? But she did not sleep on the Green again.

After she got to know other homeless people, she stayed with them. "If we all went to safe places together, we were all right. You never go off with a boyfriend because you knew he'd just try you out and then leave you. I never got involved in a situation like that.

"I got to the point where I didn't remember how food tasted. If you can't eat, you tell yourself you're not hungry. If you've got to stay awake because it's not safe to go to sleep, you tell yourself, you're not sleepy."

Like most homeless, she did not go to her family for help. Her father had died and her mother sometimes sent her a $100 or $200 money order and sometimes Josie phoned her collect. "It adds up. She's older now and she doesn't have that much money. When I was on the street, I wanted to go home but I knew she'd say 'You've got to take care of yourself. You've got a life to live. You're old enough.' She's right, in a way. Not that she was ever mean to me. Besides, I never told her I was on the street. I knew she'd be nervous."

Josie was saved from the street by Dan, whom she met in the soup kitchen. "Thank God for him. I wasn't working then but I wound up getting a job in Security and he wound up getting in Security, too. We put our money together and we had a really nice place. We did good."

She was off the street but she really didn't have a home. It was Dan's home and he started to drink. "He's a nice person but when he drinks, he messes up. He acts like a kid and starts crying or showing off, or he spends all his money on booze. I just couldn't handle it. But he helped me. So, in a way, I can't hold it against him. It always seems to happen. I always meet people who drink. I said to myself, 'Start over.'"

After that, she lived with Hank for a while but his wife decided to come back and she had to leave. By then, she had found a good job with Dandy Discounts and decided to try to get her own place. She ended by renting an apartment that was far too expensive for her. "It was the best apartment I ever had, Windsor Towers. I really did good. And I did it by myself." But she had to keep going to the soup kitchen as she was spending all her money on rent.

One evening, Mac sat down beside her. "Remember me?" He seemed a nice young man who used to come to the soup kitchen often until he left for California. Now he was back and needed a place to stay. "Just till I get myself situated." She looked at him. She had a big empty apartment. "You can stay with me, if you like," she said.

The next night he was gone with the check for $50 that her mother had sent for her birthday. It was all the money she had. "I guess he was mad because I told him I didn't want him as a boyfriend."

She took in other street people who needed a place to stay. Sometimes there were five or six people sleeping all over the floor, drinking, smoking, making noise in the hall. Of course the management found out and was furious. But she would have been evicted anyway. Dandy Discounts went bankrupt, she lost her job and she couldn't pay the rent. She was in the street again.

This time, a friend of Dan's took her in. He was gay and moved in with his boyfriend. She could stay in his place until she was evicted.

She met Ray at the soup kitchen. He was recently out of jail and he was homeless. She took him in. They weren't working, they weren't on Welfare and they were about to be evicted. They had absolutely nothing — but the soup kitchens. "That's how we survived. As for money — bottles and cans and whatever way Ray could get money legally. Sometimes, not legally. But he never hurt anybody. And now he's totally straight.

"By the grace of God — and I believe in God, I don't care what anybody says — we both got on City Welfare and I found a rental, furnished, which we could afford, and thank God I can buy my own toilet paper. I don't need to steal it from the soup kitchen like some people. But if I really needed it, I'd ask. Because I always like to be honest. We don't have to go to the kitchen every night now because we usually have food at home and we have food stamps. But sometimes it's good just to get out and have a nice meal. But if I knew there wasn't enough food and other people really needed it, I'd give it to them. Sometimes it's nice in the kitchen. If people are nice and you can all sit down and talk, then I like it. I have a few friends there and we go out together once in a while. But if you see people who are drunk and dirty, you don't want to be around them. I don't see that much. But I feel better when I know I have money and I don't really have to go.

"My ex-husband, Clyde's on the State so he only comes to the soup kitchen when he's out of money. I see the children there and sometimes I go to their house, sometimes they come to mine. They both like Ray because they know he treats me right. They've always been with their father since we first came here so they feel closer to him. That's what makes me feel bad.

"Things are all right at the moment. So I believe in God because God helped me. But if these cuts go through and we don't get jobs, we're going to lose our rent. We're going to wind up on the street again. But it's going to be worse. Nobody's going to be safe walking the streets no more. They'll have to have the National Guard out because people are going to be killing each other. And that's what the governor and the officials want. They want everybody to fight with each other and kill each other. People have no heart. They don't care. I can't believe it's going to happen. But if it does, and I don't get a job, I will go to the legislators' houses, knock on their doors peacefully, without getting arrested, and say, 'Please, let me have a job. I want to survive. I want to live.'

"Getting a job is tough. I'm used to working forty, fifty, sixty hours, but now I can't even find a part-time job. If I could, I'd take it in a minute. Then maybe Ray will feel better if he knows there's money coming in.

"Hopefully, things will work out and we'll just start over. I wouldn't ask for much. Long as we have a nice place to live and we can survive and be happy and I can have my kids back. And let them start over and be happy, too.

"So now I'm on Welfare just like that girl in the 9th grade. And my kids are, too. But I think things will work out. I believe in God, that He will help me."

MICHELLE

"If I get in a drug program, I could get my children back. And I want my children back."

She is a small, very thin African American dressed in dark, shapeless clothes: jeans, jacket and a woolen cap that completely covers her hair. She looks very young and very scared. Actually, she is thirty-two and very intelligent. She rarely comes to the soup kitchen but I found her one afternoon in the Rec Center making Easter baskets for her children. She stayed for the lecture on AIDS, joined in the discussion and announced that she was HIV positive. "I'm not ashamed of it," she said. We met at the Rec Center in the small, cold, dirty storeroom surrounded by mops, brooms, pails and boxes. She looked with interest at the broken highchair between us with the tape recorder balanced on its soiled tray.

When I was in school in South Carolina, I got a beating I'll never forget. For eating peanuts in rithmetic class. Down there they chastise kids for whatever. The parents give them permission to take you in the clothes closet and beat you with big paddles." She was about seven years old then and when she got home, she was beaten again by her great aunt. She was used to being beaten. But that day, she was angry. She phoned her grandparents and said, "Please, come get me out of this school." They came and took her back with them to New Hope. "But my grandmother, she beat me, too. Oh, yes. Believe me, yes."

She was born when her mother was sixteen and Michelle rarely saw her until she was grown. "Me and my mother had a very close relationship. She never beat me." She says it as if this were something remarkable and shows no resentment toward her mother for having abandoned her and no curiosity about her father whom she never mentions.

She had a comfortable home in New Hope with her grandparents. She had plenty of food and plenty of clothes. But when she was eleven, her grandfather, a steelworker, raped her and kept using her sexually. "It always happened when he was drunk. My grandmother was always out with different men. I told her, 'If you was home taking care of your wifely duty, what your husband did to me wouldn't have happened.' But she just looked at me like it was my fault. 'He wouldn't never do nothing like that,' she said. Wasn't no one I could talk to. My mother was never around. And come to find out, he had did the same thing to her. So it was like a hush hush thing in the family."

By the time she was thirteen, Michelle was heavily into smoking reefers, introduced to them by an older cousin. "Whenever my grandfather wanted to have sex, he would give me money to go buy reefers. So now when I have a relationship with a man, my hand is always out. 'You gottta pay me for sex.' Cause that's what he did."

She went from reefers to popping pills to drinking. "I was a teenage alcoholic. And from there I went to using drugs, selling drugs. I didn't know anything about drugs when I started. But my mother was into drugs." One day, her mother took her to see a friend of hers, a drug addict, to show her what drugs can do, hoping to scare her. But Michelle sat there fascinated. "Watching that big man with his eyes staring and his head waving back and forth, looking so happy like he was on Cloud Nine, I thought: boy, it makes him feel that good, I want to try some of that too."

Her mother was selling drugs in New Hope then. When she learned Michelle was on drugs, she thought she might as well sell them, too and make some money to buy her own. She took Michelle to Montgomery Avenue, gave her drugs and showed her what to do. Michelle reports this as if it were something any loving mother would do. "It can be dangerous on the streets," she said. "You have to know who the drug addicts are. I never made a mistake."

She was expelled from school when she was sixteen but she was hardly ever there anyway. "Only thing I liked in school was science, dissecting animals. I thought about doing it professionally at one time but I don't think I'm smart enough." Instead, she went out joyriding with Len.

"He was a very, very smart boy, a street guy, much older than me. I always dealt with guys that were much older. It was more exciting. More of a challenge. We would end up at his house and I ended up with a daughter."

They took the baby and went to Portland, Oregon. "I loved it out there. It's beautiful. So clean. And lots of air. There's drugs there but not as bad as here. There's drugs everywhere. My daughter wasn't affected by drugs but my two boys are." There is a moment's pause but she says no more about this. "Len wasn't a good father. He was on drugs, too, and selling them." Michelle worked the streets. "One day a john wanted his money back. 'My child needs food,' I told him. 'I can't afford to give you the money back.'" He had a gun and threatened to kill her. She had a knife and tried to kill him first. She was arrested for prostitution and attempted murder.

"I was scared because in New Hope, all the dirt and crime I did there, I'd never been to jail. Now I was thousands of miles from home. Are these females here going to gang rape me, like you see on TV?"

But prison, she says, was a piece of cake for her. "I go my own way, I mind my own business. Soon as I went in, I let it be known, 'You don't mess with me, I don't mess with you.' They didn't. I'm small but I scare a lot of people. Because of my mouth. My grandmother always used to tell me, 'Your mouth gonna get you in trouble.' But my mouth keeps me alive.

"They put me in a cell with this dike. I stepped out to take a shower, I come back and she had all this candy and cigarettes and stuff on my bunk. 'What's this?' I said. 'Let me tell you something right now. I'm keeping this candy because you gave it to me. I'm keeping everything you gave me. But if I even think, when I go to sleep, if I even suspect you comin up here, if you even touch my bunk by mistake, I'm gonna to kill you, hear?' I had the top bunk so I couldn't get away up there. She got her cell changed. After that, they gave me a cell to myself."

She had no money but she was energetic and resourceful. She set herself up as a hairdresser and made enough to buy the things she needed at the pharmacy: cigarettes, soap, shampoo, deodorants.

She had left the baby with some gay friends and when she got out, she had to fight to get her back. She returned to New Hope — with no money. She had used it all to buy drugs. "I think that commercial is true where the guy says: 'I work more, I do more drugs. I do more drugs, I work more.'

That's the circle." It was a circle she understood but could not break through.

"Sometimes I lived with my grandmother until she and me got into an argument because I'm very hot-headed. She always said, 'You reap what you sow.' And I said, 'You sowed me and you're reaping me. You can't blame me for what I do because I'm only copying what you do.' My grandmother will be sixty-four or sixty-five and she's still going out with men. She took me in when I came back because I was my grandfather's pet. I could no do wrong. He was still there but I wasn't afraid of him. I was grown. I could handle myself. He didn't bother me anymore."

Len was still on the streets of Portland and she went to live with LeRoy, a maintenance man at the University, another drug addict and the father of her sons. "He was good to me and the children. When he was working, I was comfortable. I didn't have to do the streets. All he wanted me to do was stay home and cook and clean. He always said, 'Keep your wife and keep her pregnant.' That was okay. Just a little boring. I was doing drugs then but I was able to take care of the kids because he made sure I had all the drugs I needed. I love my children dearly. I think I was pretty good as a mother. They were getting along all right. He would take them to school, pick them up, bring them home. Dinner would be cooked. Do the homework, go to the park, come back home, take baths, stretch out on the floor and watch TV. That was my day. I enjoyed that.

"But LeRoy wanted to be so obsessive over me. He didn't want me to go no place. I couldn't do nothing. I couldn't wear dresses, I couldn't wear make-up. When I started going around with him, this is how he preferred me to look: in jeans, sneakers, cap. That way, he wouldn't have to worry about anyone else lookin at me. I couldn't even go across the street to the store. Because when I came back, I got my behind whipped.

"And he was on drugs very heavy. One day he thought I had sneaked a guy out of the house. He dragged me outside, put a gun in my head and threatened to blow it off. Another time he snatched me out of the car and beat me so bad with a steel baseball bat. I had to get away. To this day he still threatens to kill me.

"I have a friend, a john. He's a white guy. He would drop off $60 in my mailbox every morning. Around 5:00 o'clock, he would come back, take me and my kids out to dinner and give me more money. The next morning, the same thing. So after the kids left for school, I would snatch the envelope, stick it in my housecoat and peek down the street. Are they gone? Go out the house — naked sometime with just a long coat on — run down the street, get my drugs and get back in the house. That went on for seven years. I was as skinny as this post. Nobody would never see me. I wouldn't call nobody. I stayed locked up in my house, sit in my bedroom and take drugs all day. My grandmother had the children taken away from me.

"Now I'm just starting to be with this gentleman again. But I told him, 'Look, I don't want you to give me money to buy drugs because I'm trying to cut down. You want to give me money, give me money for something positive. Take me out to dinner, take me to the movies, buy me some clothes.' Drugs I don't need. I've been off them for the last couple of days. I'm not saying if he put money in my hand tonight, what I'm going to do with it. I know what I'm going to do with it."

She lives with her grandmother on and off. The rest of the time she lives anywhere she can. "I don't go nowhere near my kids or my grandmother when I'm doin drugs. Because all I'm thinkin about is, where can I get some money. I know enough people so I don't have to sleep on the street. Like Ron's Shooting Gallery on Campbell. I can stay with him. I'm looking for a place. I'm on the City but it's very hard for a single woman to find a place.

"My grandmother's always puttin me down in front of my kids. She tells my kids I'm not their mother. My son, he looked at me the other day and he said, 'You don't buy me nothin. You don't take care of me. You're not my mommy.' I grabbed him. 'Let me tell you something. I wouldn't care if I never bought you a piece of bubble gum. I had you and nobody in this world can say they can do what I did for you.' I have a great time with my kids. They love me. But I love them to death." The only time she uses the word "love" is in connection with her children.

One of her sons was adopted and is living in Florida. He was born with asthma and bronchitis and needed special treatment. Her grandmother reported that she was unfit. "She's a dirty old bitch. I didn't agree to it. I never signed no papers. Someday I'll get him. I'll hitchhike. I'll find a way and I'll snatch my baby back."

Her friend, Ryan, works in a package store. He wasn't on drugs but he was once an alcoholic. One morning, he woke up, reached for the bottle and it MOVED. "I swear to God," he told Michelle, "every time I reached for that bottle, it moved." That was the last time he ever took a drink.

"He's a doll. He'd do anything in the world for me. I'm very fond of him. We broke up because of my drug problem. We had a beautiful apartment. I had a car, everything. I would go out, stay away for two or three days and walk back in the house, like it wasn't nothing. He put up with my mess doing that for a whole year. One day, he packed my stuff and threw it out on the street. But as long as I know he'll always be there, I can make it." This is the only time she ever admits needing anyone, and he is the only man she was ever close to who wasn't on drugs. Meeting him is the only bit of good fortune she has known. Would it have made a difference if it had happened sooner — or later?

"I'm taking money from the State and I hustle on the street. Which is not enough. I'm HIV and I don't use safe sex all the time. Which is bad. Paddy wagons go down the street, pick up the girls, take them downtown, draw blood. They stay in the lock-up till the tests come back. If you're HIV, they send you to jail. You do time. If you're clean, they let you back out. No problem. You go right back on your corner.

"I've had the virus for seven years. I been hospitalized once. I had diarrhea so bad I was bleeding. They didn't know I was HIV then. I stayed in the hospital for two weeks. The same day I got out, I went down the street to stick another needle in my arm. I'm not careful about clean needles. Who cares? I don't care.

"Let me show you something." She rolls up her sleeves and her arm is covered with scars. "That's from needles. It's not painful when you shoot it. The pain comes later. But that," she points to a big, nasty, red sore, "that's an abscess where I missed. That hurts. I won't let the nurse cut it open. I can do it myself. If I could take all the money out of my arms that I put in there with drugs, I'd be rich. I'm taking more than most because I have an ex-boyfriend that's a big drug addict. I can go over there where he's at and play lovey dovey and have all the drugs I want. It's a terrible craving. I've always been a strong person. My body can take anything."

Her mother died of AIDS the day after Mother's Day. One night, after she died, Michelle was shooting cocaine. "All of a sudden, I swear to God, her spirit or whatever, was standing in front of me. She was like holding out her arms, showing me the scars from the needles, and she says, 'You see what the drugs did to me?' I was staring up at her and that's when I messed up. I know she's dead. But she came to me. She's protecting me.

"I never denied to my children that I'm a drug addict. My daughter's thirteen, my son's seven. I told them, 'Yes, I shoot drugs. That's why Mommy doesn't come around like she should. It's a sickness that she can't control right now. It's a disease. But Mommy's trying to get it together. Just bear with me.' And my granddad looks at me like, 'You been tryin to get it together for years. When you gonna do it?'

"I like to come to the soup kitchen because it's around people. It gives me a break from the drugs. It's good because you feed a lot of people that are hungry, that really need the food. It's bad because a lot of these people are alcoholics and drug addicts and, like my grandfather keeps telling me, 'If you can scrape the money to finance shit, you can goddamn scrape it to get you something to eat in the store.' That's how I see it, too.

"What I want for my daughter? To be totally different from her mother. Whatever she wants to be, that's fine with me. We have a very good relationship. I tell her about condoms, birth control pills, all the things you need to know. I don't want her to end up like me, pushing a baby carriage down the street at... I don't even know when. I been pregnant so many times and had so many abortions.

"Kids need to have sex education and drug education in school but it depends on the individual. I can't say I would have been saved by it. I'm the type of person, if you say, 'That's bad,' I'm gonna find out for myself. Like my mother used to say, 'If so and so jumped off that bridge, you gonna jump too?' Yes, cause I want to see the thrill of it.

"My son wants to be a cop and clean up all the drugs. He said, 'If I clean up all the drugs, I don't have to worry about no one else's Mommy bein on drugs.' Makes me feel so bad." She stares at the dirty highchair and her face, which has been without expression, becomes suddenly twisted. She begins to cry. I get up and put my arms around her. "I haven't never talked my frustrations, my true feelings out like this in a long time. I'm a very quiet person till they hit that wrong nerve.

"I'm trying to get in a drug program. I have accepted the fact that I have a drug habit and I know I don't have it under control. I always taught myself, there's nothing in this world you can't do if you put your mind and heart to doin it. If I get in a program, I could get my children back. And I want my children. When you come back from England in the fall, I'll be a new person. You won't even know me. The only way will be by my voice. And I'll have my own home then, with my children in it.

"The worst that can happen to me, I can die. I can OD. I'm not goin to the doctor the way I should. I just received a letter stating that I should get in touch with him pronto, concerning my health. And I still haven't picked up the phone and called. If I could live over again, I would go to college. I'd like to be a surgeon. I'd like to cut people up. I have a very steady hand. I would know when to stop. Long as there wasn't anybody down there I didn't like." She grins.

"But nobody's beating me anymore. They beat me, they better watch out."

THE ARTISTS

"... the desire of the moth for the star."

— *SHELLEY*

Gary (poet)
Kenneth (classical pianist)

I found art — loosely interpreted — in the soup kitchens, among the desperately poor and the homeless. Only two interviews are given here but there are others for whom art is of great importance.

Eric, an industrial engineer by profession, has always done a great deal of painting as well as photography and choral singing. Painting is now all he has left of his old life though he still sings, occasionally, with the New Hope Choral. He continues to paint in his tiny room though it is cramped and dark, and in spite of increasing pains in his wrist and hands.

Walter, an elderly, unemployed man, is a consumer rather than a creator, a reader rather than a writer. But he has raised reading to a fine art. It is both an occupation and a hobby. He reads all day in the University library, escaping from the soup kitchen and the uncongenial society around him. His range is exceptionally wide, from Dante to Dickens, from

Molière to Maupassant, from Hobbes to Heidegger, and he reads fluently in several languages, including Latin which he taught himself. When I ask what he is reading, his face lights up and, for a few moments in the midst of the noisy kitchen, he talks with enthusiasm and intelligence of Schopenhauer or Balzac or Octavio Paz.

Gary, like so many of our guests, has worked at many different jobs but is now unemployed. Through the influence of PEOPLE FIRST, he wrote letters to the newspaper about the plight of the unemployed and the homeless which were published in the *New Hope Mail.* Soon he was writing poems which were also published and a whole new world was opened to him. I had given him a tape of poetry readings and he reports that he intends to go on writing poems and listening to poetry on his Walkman. The excitement of discovering and writing poetry has given him a new interest and a new identity.

Music is, quite literally, Kenneth's whole life and has always been. He plays it, reads it and listens to it constantly: on a piano, on his radio, in his head. He endured terrible years on the street when, instead of music, he heard vicious voices inside his head commanding him to do terrible things to himself. Now that he is cured, he is not in the least bitter about those painful, wasted years. Rather, he feels lucky because he has music again, as he says, in his ears and at his fingertips.

Each of these men has managed to reach beyond the narrow and humiliating limits of the soup kitchen.

GARY

He is a thoughtful, energetic African American who sometimes wears horn-rimmed glasses and sometimes a large cowboy hat, reflecting his dual nature. He is very warm, friendly and outgoing, loves sports and has a capacity for enjoying life. But he displays a serious streak as well, with a desire to achieve, has something of a social conscience and an undeveloped interest in poetry. He has written several good letters to the papers protesting the cuts in Welfare and several poems which were all published. I gave him an audio tape of poetry readings and he seemed extremely pleased though surprised that they didn't all rhyme. He named several that he especially liked.

My parents were Baptists, but I decided to go to a Catholic school because my friends all went to public schools and they seemed to be just havin fun. I wanted to be serious. I wanted to get a better education and I heard the Catholic schools were better." He worked in the school kitchen to pay for his tuition: waiting on tables, washing dishes, cleaning up. "It was easy."

There were only five African Americans in the whole school but there was no racism, no trouble of any kind. He went to school dances, pitched for the baseball team, played Varsity basketball, ran the 8/80, shot pool, played ping pong and bowled. "I was always busy. I like being busy. I had a lotta friends. I had a great time." He didn't mind that church was compulsory, that there were classes in religion and catechism. He loved math but it was the English teacher who made the deepest impression. Mr. Stanford was a small man with wispy hair. "Everybody made fun of him because he always wore the same tan suit and the same brown tie every day. But he knew so much about English literature: about Shakespeare and poetry and prose. I used to talk to him a lot. I was impressed by him because he was his own man when it came to English literature. And he was a very good teacher. We wrote a lot of English papers in his class and we read a lot of poetry. I can still remember *The Raven.* I liked that. That class was really good. It was always exciting."

Gary lived in an integrated neighborhood with white neighbors on both sides. "Their children were all good friends of mine. I saw them after school. We had a great time." His father was a workaholic. During the week, he was a painter and paperhanger and boasted that he hung the best corners in town. He taught Gary how to do it, too. On weekends, he played in his own band, all over the state. "We were the first Blacks in town to have a '57 Chevy convertible," Gary said. His father died, Gary claimed, from overwork when Gary was thirteen.

"After graduation, I wanted to get out of town, get away, so I went to San Francisco where my oldest sister was teaching. I got a job with the American Can Company and then with a bank in stock transfers. They taught me. It was a sort of on the job training. I liked it. But I had a drug problem.

"All my friends were smoking marijuana. They had 'smoke-ins' where people sat in a circle in someone's apartment and smoked all day. I did, too. Whenever we had time off, we smoked. I was missing a lot of time at work." In the end, he lost his job.

The Black Panthers moved to town and Gary joined them. "We initiated grocery clubs and breakfasts for school kids. I liked being part of it. It was exciting and I felt we were doing something constructive, something important to help poor Blacks, something no one else was doing."

Gary stopped taking drugs when he became involved with the Panthers. "It was hard but I got a lot of help from them. They made me see that Blacks who did drugs were doing the white man a big favor; making him rich and destroying themselves all by themselves. The white man didn't have to lift a finger or a gun. All he had to do was sit back, watch the process and rake in the money. I never used drugs again."

He finally got a job through a girlfriend, Odelle, whose uncle sold beauty supplies in San Diego, California. While Gary was there, he met the man who invented the California Curl for black people. "I didn't know black people needed something special to make their hair curl. But Odelle said you straightened it first and then you curled it. To make it look like white people's. She said he was a hero to his race. He still had his first little barber shop right in front of his factory, to let people know where he came from."

Gary learned a lot about hairdressing. "It was okay. But helping black people make their hair look more like white people's didn't seem the way to go. I wondered what the Panthers would think."

He did a lot of other jobs, too, such as all the maintenance work on the three houses he and Odelle owned. They lived in one and rented the other two. Gary bought a truck and hired three men to help with outside painting while he did the inside work, painting and hanging wallpaper like his father. "I paid them pretty well and it gave them something to do, kept them off the streets." He also drove a school bus two or three days a week as a substitute driver. He was, as he had been in school, busy all the time.

"We even took care of Odelle's auntie that was ninety years old. She used to work as a maid for the people that owned the St. Louis Cardinals and she had a baseball signed with all the players' names. My mother's into baseball real hard so when Odelle's auntie gave me the ball, I gave it to my mother with its own little stand. It's about twenty or thirty years old. And she still has it."

All of a sudden business got bad. Black people seemed to stop worrying about their hair. They even stopped worrying about their houses so the paint and paper-hanging work stopped, too. The city still needed school bus drivers but there wasn't much money in that. "Looked like the recession had already started only nobody knew it — except the Blacks; the last hired and the first fired. All of a sudden, I wasn't busy anymore."

He went to New Hope because he thought there would be more work there and got a job with Sal's Pizza as a delivery man. He drove all over Rhode Island, Connecticut and parts of New York State, delivering pizza to all the big food chain stores. He had a different route every day. He enjoyed that, enjoyed being outdoors on his own, looking at the countryside, watching it change from one town to the next, from one month to the next; looking at grass and trees instead of litter and billboards and homeless people with their hopeless stare. "I think that's what I'd like to do permanently, drive a delivery van — way out of the city, even out of the state."

He was expecting Odelle to move out to New Hope with him. He sent her $200 for the fare — and she sent it back. She had a new boyfriend.

One day, he went to Manchester with Mr. Baker, his boss. Gary drove the huge trailer truck because Mr. Baker had his license suspended for drunken driving. On the highway, they were stopped by the state police and Gary got a ticket. He didn't have a license for driving that huge truck. He was told to come back in two weeks to take a special test that would cost $40.00. He was fired. "We'll have to let you go," Mr. Baker said. "You do a good job, we'd like to keep you. But we've got to move that pizza." Though it was Baker, with his drunken driving, who was to blame, it was Gary who was punished. Mr. Baker never even offered to pay for that special license.

Gary couldn't find another job. That was a shock. "I'd never been out of work before." But now the recession was hitting the white community, too. No one was hiring. His unemployment payments ran out. He had to go on Welfare. He moved to the Y. Luckily, he still had some money and could pay cash so he got in easily. The Y didn't want Welfare recipients anymore because their rental allowance had been cut from $325 to $200 and they couldn't make up the difference. And the city was threatening to cut it even further.

Gary thought the Y would be a nice place to live, with a gymnasium and a swimming pool and a restaurant. But the restaurant was padlocked, the swimming pool had no water and the gym was closed because it wasn't insured. "Meanwhile, they're still taking our money and all that equipment is just sitting there, going to waste."

A crew from Workfare did the cleaning. "They can't choose their work. Welfare assigns the jobs and they can't make any money so it's not like having a real job. They're just putting in time." The place was full of roaches. One day, Gary's next door neighbor had a roach crawl into his ear. They had to take him to the hospital to get it out.

"Most of the tenants seem like mental patients, dumped there when they closed the hospitals. They shoot drugs and drink all the time. They break into rooms, steal TVs, things like that. They broke the lights in the halls so you have to walk around in the dark. It's dangerous. I got involved in one fight. Worse, most of the people there have just given up."

One day, coming back from a job interview in a suit and hat, he met one of the older tenants going out. "'Man, lookee you,' he said. 'You still draggin your ass round tryin to find a job? They hire you this time? Course they didn't. Like they didn't hire you last time or the time before that. Like they ain't gonna hire you next time neither. But some fools never learn.' It's a depressing place to live.

"But there were some good people there. I made some friends." He learned about the soup kitchen from them. "I like to go, whether I eat or not. I can help clean up or help someone with a form or a resumé. There are a lot of good people there. We have a lot in common so we help each other. But a few are pretty wild, pushing ahead, coming through the line two and three times before seconds are served, grabbing food off other people's plates. The people in charge just leave them alone because they don't want a confrontation."

Through the soup kitchen, he became involved with PEOPLE FIRST. He goes to meetings and demonstrations and helps with distributing flyers. "I had a little experience with the Panthers. What I'd really like to do is get the University more involved. Get some money from them since they're part of the problem. With the city so broke, they could at least pay taxes."

One day one of the volunteers in the soup kitchen, a University student, invited him to speak to a group of students about the homeless. He felt very nervous, standing in front of a classroom with twenty white students staring up at him. They knew nothing about unemployed and homeless people, though they walked right past them every day on their way to the bank next door to a soup kitchen. "Taking out money for restaurants and movies and discos and liquor and holiday trips, money the unemployed need for food and clothes," Gary said. He tried to tell the students what it was like not to have a job, not to have a home, not to have enough cash for a haircut or a bus ride or a phone call. And almost no hope of ever getting any.

He told them about that social worker at the Welfare office who made him come back six times. "'You didn't fill the form out.' 'Today is the sixth, not the fifth.' 'It says put down your *full* name' 'But my name don't come any fuller,' I said. 'You neglected to include your zip code. You left out the comma after the day of the week. You left out the period after the year.' She kept filling out papers on her desk while she said it. Kept me waiting six weeks for my Welfare check. There are a lot like her."

Sitting in his room at the Y one night, listening to the shouting around him and feeling very low, he wrote a letter to the newspaper:

> I want a job and I want a fair share for my brothers and sisters. We are trying hard but we don't seem to be getting anywhere. We keep our work shoes on and keep putting in applications that collect dirt like our shoes. At Temporary Labor we sit all morning and maybe two or three fellows get a temporary job that pays $3 or $4 an hour while regular workers get $12 to $14 an hour.
>
> You get paid by check that can only be used at the company store which charges another fee for cashing it. They also deduct the fare for driving you to the worksite. You have just enough money to get you to Temporary Labor the next day. To be degraded again. We might as well sign up for Disability for we are disabled in the workplace.

The letter was published. But Gary is still unemployed.

There are many things he can do and has done: drive a truck, drive a school bus, paint, hang wallpaper, even work in business as he did with the beauty supply company. But he can find nothing. "Not even a volunteer job, like coaching basketball. I like basketball and I like kids. I tried the Boys' Club and the Police Pals and the Y. I even tried Head Start. Nothing. Finally, The Salvation Army took me on as a volunteer around Christmas time, driving their truck. But that only lasted a few weeks. So now I'm not only an unemployed worker, I'm an unemployed volunteer. It's hard to believe because I've always been busy. I like being busy. I think I'm a good worker. But right now I'm nothing."

If the Welfare cuts go through, his situation will be even worse. The new law stipulates that, after six months, the benefits stop. "And I've been out of work for nine months already. Sometimes I feel like I'll never work again. I'll just be standing on the corner of Clay and Clark holding a paper cup, watching the students pass by right in front of me. But they won't see me. They'll be looking at something else. Just like that social worker."

He wrote other letters to the newspaper and they were published, too. "They were coming out in a more poetic form, so I decided to turn them into poems. I thought Mr. Stanford, my old English teacher, would like that. I like writing poems. I like listening to that tape you gave me with people reading poetry on it. Sometimes I listen to it in my room or sitting on the Green. If I ever get that job again, making deliveries, I would buy more tapes and listen to them in the truck. I could even start making up poems in my head while I drive. I think they'd be different from the ones I write now. I have a new poem. It's called 'Hope after Dope.' So far, I've written three and they've all been published. I sent them home to my mother. I think that baseball with the autographs on it and my poems are her most valuable possessions. I'm glad she doesn't know I had to borrow money for the stamps."

KENNETH

"All I wanted to do was play the piano."

He is a quiet, pleasant white man, well-spoken and nice-looking though he is missing several front teeth and his hair is cropped and jagged. "I cut it myself. It looks it." His jacket is too tight and his jeans too short. "I was given these clothes just recently, all of them — jacket, trousers, shirt, socks and shoes — by one of my old piano students. They're the first clothes I've worn since 1986 that I didn't find in garbage cans." He is fifty-one, a classical pianist with degrees from The Cleveland Institute and the Carlyle University School of Music. He has performed both in recitals and with orchestras such as the Cleveland Symphony, and taught at Carlyle University and the Juilliard School of Music.

The first time I saw or heard a piano was in church when I was about three or four. I loved it. If I sat very still, I was allowed to play it after the service. And then, suddenly, when I was around six, a piano appeared in our living room. I sat down on the bench and I've been there, virtually, ever since." But the homeless do not have pianos.

He has only one brother but the house was always full of children, foster children. "I was never alone. There was always a crib in my room with some child in it. I liked living with all those children. I like children — of all ages."

His father was an editor on the *Cleveland News* with a small but very good private library. Kenneth read right through it. "My father worked all the time — at the typewriter. And I work all the time — at the piano. I guess I get it from him. But that's what we all do, isn't it? Work. Get up in the morning and work till it's time to go to sleep. Then get up and start working again." Yet he has been unable to work for several years.

Walking downtown, the day after he finished high school, he saw a sign that read: "Cleveland Institute of Music." He went in and heard pianos, lots of pianos. A white-haired man appeared and asked what he was doing. "Listening," he said. He was invited into a large office with a beautiful, big Steinway grand, standing quietly all by itself. "Want to play it?" He did. The man was the dean of the school and offered Kenneth a partial scholarship.

To pay for the rest of his tuition, he worked at a drive-in restaurant from about 4:30 till midnight and then got up at 6:30 in the morning to go to school. But he couldn't do this and study music, too, so the job had to go. Friends from the Institute took him in — two nights here, two nights there — and kept him alive with sandwiches and milk. Later he taught piano at the Phyllis Wheatley School for poor, black children. "Most of my teaching has been at places like that. I've taught all ages, from three up. It came easily. I think my background at home with all those foster children was very good experience for this. I enjoyed it. I believe most children are talented. I didn't feel it was an interruption to my studies. Teaching is part of being a musician."

At last he was able to pay for a room. "It cost $5.00 a week and was so small I had to hang my clothes up sideways. I had to eat out so there wasn't much money left over for movies or cigarettes. I didn't mind. There was always the piano."

He loved the Institute, so different from high school which bored him. "Here we were all interested in the work. The school was our social life, too. There were no dances. Musicians never have dances. I certainly didn't miss them. All I wanted to do was play the piano."

After graduation, he went to New York with a suitcase tied up in a belt and $14.00 in his pocket. Again, he was saved by friends. They took him in and helped him get jobs. "But there was one period when I ended up cooking beans under the hot water tap." Soon he was very busy as a teacher at Bronx House and The Henry Street Settlement, and as a freelance performer which he found terribly strenuous. "You don't have time to practice. All you can do is read the music."

He received a scholarship to the Carlyle Music School. "I didn't like it as much as the Institute but the students were great. Students always are. I learned more from them — at the Institute and at Carlyle — than from the faculty." He also taught undergraduates. "They were quite bright but they weren't musicians. They were Carlyle students who wanted to play the piano. I was paid handsomely by Carlyle." He taught at The Ridgeway, a local music school, as well and finally he had his own private students.

"I was a very successful teacher. I'm very good at technical problems. I always left the fees up to the students. Which was fine when I had lots of students. But I ended up with ten because I actually worked myself out of business. Students who had started when they were very young, quit when they went to high school because they were more interested in physics or football than the C major scale." Some quit when they went to college. Students from The Carlyle Music School were around for only two years. Others became teachers themselves so the word-of-mouth recommendations stopped. Some, whom he had been urging to go on for their masters, finally did and he lost them, too. "All of a sudden, I had no students, no income, nothing. I put my nice, new Steinway D out on consignment."

While he was going through all this, he began to hear voices. "They shouted at me to do terrible things to myself, like 'Cut off your right fingers. Jump in front of that bus.' I woke up one night and realized there was something wrong with my ears. I was hearing strange sounds. I thought two of my long-time students had taken me to the hospital while I was asleep and put transistors into my ears in place of my eardrums. It changed the natural ear into something electronic."

Once he played for the president of Steinway in New York who was thinking of booking him. "I hadn't prepared very well so I was scared. Suddenly, that man's voice began yelling inside my head, 'Get those pieces in your fingers. Dammit. Get them in your fingers.' I began to play — Chopin and Debussy — but all I heard was that voice.

"I walked around the streets of New Hope, digging my fingers into my ears, trying to figure out what was wrong and crying because I thought that two of six students had done this to me. I had never been out of work before. I'd been teaching since I was seventeen. I didn't know about shelters or soup kitchens. I didn't know about homelessness or Welfare or

Unemployment Benefits. It was terrible. Everything happened at once. I lost my students, my home, my piano. And the voices kept at me, telling me to do this, do that."

He was on the streets for about two years, sleeping under trees, in doorways and under an old couch in a ditch near the cemetery. "It rains and you get soaked. It's very cold and you're sure you'll freeze to death. Of course, you have to be very careful not to sleep outside fancy restaurants or hotels. Sometimes I slept in the railway station but it was very cold even there. Cold is something that terrifies me. The police would wake me up and I'd leave. Most of the time, I'd hide behind one of those huge dumpsters in back of the station or *in* one, where I'd be protected from the wind, and pray that the garbage truck wouldn't come too early in the morning. Finding water was one of the worst problems. For washing and laundry, you had to use snow or jump into the creek or the river. But drinking water was almost impossible to find.

"I used to go to MacDonald's — and every restaurant along the way — at 4:00 AM to poke through their garbage, with the voices taunting, scolding, threatening to kill me. It was like being captured by the enemy and tortured, literally tortured, steadily and without end." Like many of the homeless, he never thought of going home or asking friends for help. And he never joined any of the other street people. "There was one fellow who wanted to know my name because, he said, I looked like a portrait by Holbein. I think he was a Harvard graduate. There was another fellow who'd been living in a van for years. He would drive down the street, calling to people through a bullhorn. I stayed as far away from other people as possible. I lived, so to speak, with my head down.

"There's something called pride. Some people don't want to go home and they don't want to go on Welfare. They will struggle to make it on their own. Some people prefer the street to a shelter. They want to stay outdoors. They have these little places that they make for themselves. There are some people like that in the soup kitchen. They manage. They don't care about washing their clothes. The rain does that or they get new clothes from the soup kitchen. For some people, the soup kitchen is all they have. But some don't even go there. They go to the garbage cans. Like me.

"I hated to ask for money. I'd always been independent. But I did — twice. People have been very kind. One man gave me 75¢, another gave me a couple of dollars. Once a man saw me rummaging in a trash can and gave me $5.00. I didn't want to take it but he insisted.

"Every now and then, I'd come to and find myself poking through garbage cans and I'd be horrified. What am I doing here? Why am I doing this? In my saner moments, I thought I had brain cancer or some other terrible disease and that I was going to die. I decided to travel. I wanted to see all my friends before that happened."

He still had a little money from the sale of his piano which he was saving, hoping he could buy it back. Instead, he took a bus to New York, San Francisco, Los Angeles, Cleveland, Chicago. "If you live on the street, you can live anywhere — on any street. If you have no job, no family, you have no responsibilities. You can always start over again somewhere else. I think it's an attitude many homeless people develop. Sometimes I worked in those temporary workplaces but I was still sleeping out."

He slept in divided highways with grass down the middle where the police couldn't see him in the dark. In San Francisco, he slept in dumpsters, one filled with clumps of sponge rubber, another with old rugs. They helped keep him warm. "Once I found a dumpster outside a bakery loaded with garbage — including bread. That was a windfall."

In Cleveland, he lived for a whole winter in an abandoned truck with no heat but he found some insulation and put that in the cab. "There were nights when I was afraid to fall asleep for fear I'd never wake up. One night I found a sleeping bag in the truck. Somebody must have left it for me. I opened it up and there was a piece of cloth sewn into the lining which said, 'Jesus Saves.' Then my voices began to shout it over and over again: 'Jesus Saves. Jesus Saves.' I hadn't been to church since I was a child."

Finally, when he was more than half wild from the voices and the cold, he walked up to a policeman and said "Take me to the hospital." The hospital gave him therapy and put him on medications. But what it mainly did was to keep him off the streets during the very cold weather. "I don't know how long I was there. My sense of time and chronology during my sickness and while I was on the streets — with no watch, no calendar, no newspapers, no radio — was very warped."

He worked at Temporary Labor in Cleveland, earning the minimum wage of $4.50 an hour, less taxes (though the employer paid Temporary Labor $8.00, in lieu of insurance and medical care). He earned $20.00 a day and spent $20.00 a day — for food and a room. Finally he was off the street. But just.

"It was all factory work. There was no training. Just bad jobs. Dirty jobs. Dangerous jobs. Very dangerous. Jobs that the regular employees refused to do. We worked with industrial saws, power saws, punch presses, things of that sort. There were stories of people getting their fingers cut off. I was very nervous about my hands." He was living in a room about as big as a kitchen table with hardly enough space to open and close the door. "This took just about all my earnings. If my voices got too bad and I couldn't work, which happened every now and then, I'd lose even that."

One night he was walking across a bridge, walking home after a Temporary Labor job. His head hurt terribly and he was crying out loud with the pain and the sense of complete hopelessness. Suddenly, in the middle of the bridge, he heard his voices shouting, "Jump. Jump." He stopped. He wanted to jump. He tried to jump. But he couldn't. The next day, walking back to the Temporary Labor office very early in the morning, he saw two policemen standing on the bridge where he had stood the night before. There was a pea jacket on the ground and a tugboat just below with a sailor shouting that there was a man in the water. "I felt terrible, as if I had pushed him in myself."

In Chicago, he got a job in a restaurant but was paid only every two weeks so, for the first two weeks, he had to live on the street. "I hid a blanket in the bushes so the boss wouldn't know and, after working till 1:30 in the morning, I would pick it up and try to find a place where the police wouldn't catch me. The nicest places were the cemeteries because no one goes there. I don't remember where I got the blanket. In San Francisco, they throw them on the streets for the homeless."

In the restaurant, he washed dishes. "I liked that. It's fast, clean work. But my voices were giving me trouble. This time I thought there were soldiers out there and they were aiming some kind of weapon at me. I thought they had the microwave antennae connected to my head. They followed me everywhere, shouting orders, crazy things like: 'Kill the nurse,' 'Burn the books,' threatening to break my thumbs, cut off my hands, drown my piano. Luckily, I never talked out loud to myself or behaved strangely. To the outside world, I was pretty normal. But I remember crying myself to sleep because the pain in my head was so excruciating.

"Finally, the voices told me to quit the job and go back to Cleveland to see my brother because he was sick. I went. My parents had died but my brother was fine. He had inherited my parents' house and land because I wasn't there when they died. He also owned a carpet business. He clearly didn't want me around. The voices were pretty bad the whole time I was with him."

Somehow Kenneth landed in New York where the police told him about Bedford Stuyvesant, an armory that had been converted into a huge shelter. "It was full of tough-looking people. They had guards at the door — lots of guards — with guns and a metal detector. Every time you walked in or out, they opened your pack and checked it for guns and knives and any kind of metal. When I went upstairs that first night, the guys on my floor pointed to a bed and said, 'Over there.' They were enormous, muscle-bound beings. They worked out like crazy, throwing the heavy chairs across the room. It was like a prison and they ran it. Most of them had just gotten out of jail anyway. I felt very threatened by them. I tied my shoes together and put some of the castors from the chairs by my bed.

"They made me leave my pack outside the dining hall where I knew it would be stolen. It was. That means I had no clothes, no money and no identification of any kind — birth certificate, driver's license, nothing. The Shelter helps you apply for new ones but it takes about six weeks to get them. And as soon as they come, your pack is stolen again. It happened to me many, many times. In shelters, on buses, everywhere."

Coming home one night, he suddenly found himself on the ground while two men ripped his pockets all the way down on both sides, looking for his wallet. One sat on his legs and the other stood over his head. "I didn't know whether I was going to be beaten up or killed or what. Finally one of them said, 'Did you get it?' and I felt a bang on my head. There were about forty people standing around in total silence. Finally they went into the Shelter with me, banged on the door and said, 'Let this guy in. He's been attacked and robbed. We know who it is and you guards know who it is.' But the guards were not interested.

"I went upstairs where a huge female guard was on duty. She stood looking at me with my pants ripped down, my shirt in a mess and the blood pouring from my head. 'Howya doin?' she said."

He came back to New Hope — to Jefferson House, a private shelter. He had no money, no job, no home, no Welfare. "Jefferson House takes you in, gives you a bed, two meals, toothpaste and soap. We washed our clothes in the sinks at night. They move you around constantly so you don't feel it's your home or even your bed. You have to apply every night. During the day, you wander around, trying to stay in crowded places such as the Mall, trying to stay warm and inconspicuous.

"The other people in the Shelter were fine. People are people. It was peaceful. There wasn't any fighting or stealing in Jefferson House itself. But in the Annex, I was robbed and attacked several times: punched on the arm, in the head, in the neck. Because someone didn't like me or because I sat in the wrong place, or because I took someone's chair. Steam builds up in people and finally they lash out at anybody.

"Jefferson House helped me find a place to live, helped me get on Welfare and helped me get medical care. Finally, I was off the street."

Now he has a tiny room, paid for by the city. "It's very well-painted and it's light. It's really great. At first, the only thing in the room was a thin mattress and a little dresser. Everything else: the bed, the springs, the chairs — I have a great steel chair that I use for practicing — my bedding, my clothes, I found in garbage cans. Every two weeks I get $54 from Welfare which means I have $25 every week for food or whatever else I want. I bought some cigarettes today, which is the first pack in ages. Otherwise, I roll my own. Of course I have no money for barbers and I certainly can't afford a dentist. My teeth look it.

"I do some work in the house. I'm the only one who does. I wash all the dishes, take the garbage out, do all the vacuuming. Some people in the house are mentally ill, like Julie, my next door neighbor. She rarely comes out of her room, except to go to the bathroom or to the kitchen to make tea. She never cooks. She's afraid someone will poison her food if she puts it in the refrigerator so she keeps it all in her room. She writes me angry notes, accusing me of all kinds of things: making obscene phone calls (I don't have a phone), hiding her mail (she never gets any). Once she called the police and told them I kept breaking into her room whenever she was out and changing all her clocks. She has six. Some of the residents are noisy and they're not particularly friendly but they're not threatening. The heat's good. Bathroom facilities are great. I have a key to my room. I feel safe. My landlady has given me a radio so I can listen to a classical music station. What's to complain about?

"I don't need to go to soup kitchens three times a day anymore but I still go occasionally. In the beginning, I felt ashamed to go. But I don't feel that way now. You can't go on being ashamed all your life. I think the people who run it are very kind, very nice. I don't have any problems with the other guests. The only thing about it is that there are very few people there who have anything in common with me so I feel like an outsider. But they treat me all right.

"I've always gone to libraries and museums, even during my sickness and I go now. I love art, have since I was twelve. I even used to paint. When I was at the Cleveland Institute, The Cleveland Museum was right down the street so I went there all the time. It's small but they have some exquisite things. Like the 12th century enamels. I've read a lot of art history, Jansen, Delacroix's journal, and a lot about music. I've just finished a book from the public library on the age of Louis XIV. I have to know all kinds of things for my students, such as performance practices in earlier periods. Besides, if you play a phrase in a certain way, you have to have a reason for it. But there's been no music in my life for a long time now — except, recently, through the radio and reading. Earlier, when I read music, I could always hear it inside my head. And now that the voices have gone, I can do that again; I find I can listen to whatever I want inside my head again. I don't need to go to concerts. I can even practice pieces in my head.

"I haven't heard the voices for almost a year now. The doctor says this disease can affect anyone from any economic background. He thinks I'll probably never have this problem again. I feel pretty secure about that as long as I've got a decent place to live. I know that some of the people on the street are sick. Probably some are there because they're sick. But I think that some are sick because they're *there.*"

Now that he no longer hears voices, he has made contact with some of his old students and friends again. "They take me out for coffee and dinner. It's hard because I don't like to take. I can give very easily but it's difficult for me to take. I want to earn my own money in my own way. You'll find that's true of a lot of the people in the soup kitchens.

"Right now, I'm looking for students. I'm sending out letters and resumés to lots of music schools. I'd like to put an ad in the newspaper but that's expensive. In the meantime, I hope to find a job as a dishwasher or something of that sort. I learned to type at the library so maybe I can work as a secretary or a file clerk.

"I have four recitals coming up with a singer who's hired me to accompany her — for pay! I study the score and we practice at her house on Saturday afternoons. The music is technically easy. And it's great to be playing the piano again.

"But now there is a time pressure I never felt before. I've lost too many teeth."

THE MILITARY

"Soldiers are citizens of death's grey land..."

— SIEGFRIED SASSOON

Al (professional soldier)
Ray (Vietnam veteran)

Many of the men in the soup kitchens have served in the military, some in war time, some in peace time, as a means of escape: from home, from school, from boredom. Gordon enlisted to be with his best friend but also to escape from the restrictions of home and the boredom of college. "It was something to do," Eric said. Tyler, a member of a huge family, said, "Maybe growing up with all those people around me made me restless."

A few enlisted because they knew they would be drafted anyway. "To get it out of the way," Morgan said, "and to be able to chose my job." Pete hoped to get some technical training in the military.

Only a few mentioned travel as a reason for enlisting. Yet the others all enjoyed seeing other countries which gave them a new perspective on life in the United States. African Americans commented on the friendliness they found in England compared to the racial prejudice they experienced in America. Some were struck by the more aesthetic aspects of life outside the United States. Pete and Morgan, who drove around Germany, found it beautiful. "Everything was so clean and peaceful and quiet. They don't have billboards or trash or slums," Pete noted. "The Germans are pretty good people," Morgan reported. "They wrap their garbage up and things like that. Not like they do over here where they just pitch it." Seth appreciated the small English town of Portsmouth as well as the colorful scenes in London. James loved England. "I liked getting away from America," he said. Lonnie was struck by the beauty of the Philippines. Even Al, the professional soldier, acquired new insights into the United States.

Seth, who saw some action in Vietnam, discovered that 80% of the men in the front lines were African Americans and other minorities. All remarked on the widespread use of drugs in the military and the racial tensions. No one learned a skill he could use in civilian life. Morgan was not able to choose the kind of job he would get and Pete did not get the technical training he requested. "They were saving it for the Whites," he said.

Most of the men were very young when they joined and most claimed that the military had changed them — not for the better. Gordon could no longer live at home with his authoritarian father and Tyler was more restless than ever. Gordon was introduced to drugs in the military and some reported a noticeable increase in their drug and alcohol abuse as a result of the war. Both the men interviewed here saw heavy combat duty. Both were badly wounded and both experienced the serious problems that were part of army life in Vietnam. But the impact on each was different. Al was proud of his Service in the Green Berets and stayed in the Service.

Ray was quickly disillusioned about the war. But for both, the war had drastic, long-term effects. Both have nightmares and are given to outbreaks of violence. Both have serious alcohol and drug problems. Ray's personality changed completely — for the worse — and his life with it. Al came back with a hatred for all Asians which he fought to overcome. In the end, he was disillusioned about the Service — and even about the United States.

For both men, the effects of the Vietnam War continued far on into civilian life.

AL

"You die physically or you die mentally.
I've died mentally."

He is a brawny white man, with dark, wiry hair, a small bald spot like a bottle cap on the crown of his head and a booming voice. He moves quickly, speaks quickly, has a quick temper and is sometimes extremely bossy. But he likes to joke and creates a lively, friendly atmosphere around him. He used to come to the soup kitchen in bits of army uniform but he now dresses rather formally in trousers and shirt, perhaps to go with the new business he is planning. He makes passionate speeches against the Welfare cuts every night. He talks tough but is, at times, surprisingly emotional and compassionate. At a candlelight rally for the homeless one moonlit night, one of the men suddenly stepped inside the circle of candles. He had a serious speech defect, has been unemployed for many years and is likely to remain so. "Dear God," he began, raising his arms to the moon, "please send us jobs. Please… help us. Please." He broke down and staggered, weeping, around the circle until he fell into Al's open arms.

I'm military from way back. My real father was in the Service, my adoptive father was in the Service, my adoptive brother was in the Service, my oldest son is in the Service and I've been in the Service most of my life. You might say I've got the military coming out of my ears — or rather my hair. I think that's why I'm going bald so early — from tension and twenty-four years of active duty: in Vietnam and Cambodia and Panama and everywhere else. I started fighting as a boy, even in my own family. I enjoyed it. Could be it's in the blood because my mother was a White Apache Indian and my father was part French Canadian and part Dakota Indian. So I'm really more American than most."

He was adopted at the age of five by his godparents when his natural parents were killed in a car crash. His father and godfather had been buddies in the Marine Corps and his adoptive parents treated him like their own son. But the rest of the family resented him. They were second generation Italians and regarded him as an outsider. "I had to fight them constantly. It was a large, crooked, underhanded, Mafioso-type family except for my father who was honest and hard-working, and ran his own successful construction business. But they were all fun to be with. And they had a good relationship. If anyone got into a jam, the rest were there to help him. Except for me. I had to take care of myself."

They lived in Manhattan, in Little Italy, which was Mafia-controlled. The neighborhood was all one big happy family. There were lots of parties, lots of drugs and lots of alcohol. Al, like the other boys, started to drink when he was eleven and went on to pot and acid, but continued to drink as well. The "family" was involved in numbers and prostitution but not drugs which they thought of as a fad that would die out. Even as a boy, Al was aware of all that.

"My father wanted to be in the 'country' so he moved his family and his business to Hamden, Connecticut, which was more 'country' than Manhattan, New York. I went to work for him, after school and all day Saturday and from 9:00 to 2:00 on Sundays — and kept up a good social life, too. I was bringing home about $250 a week. I could keep the money I made so I put a lot in the bank and the rest went for drugging and drinking and partying. I was introduced to drugs by my older cousins. That cost me a lot.

"In school, I was about a C average, except in American History where I got straight As. Especially when we got down to the subject of the American Indian. I had done a lot of digging and I was in contact with my grandfather, even visited him on his reservation in New Mexico. What really got me interested was a discussion at school about George Armstrong Custer at Little Big Horn. It didn't tell why all the Indians were massed against him. It didn't tell that Custer rode into a village full of old men and women and children and ordered the extermination of each and every one of them while the warriors were five hundred miles away. It didn't tell that this village happened to be Sitting Bull's village. *That* was my favorite subject."

He enlisted in the army after graduation — he would have been drafted anyway — and did three years of training in about seven months. "I did Airborne, I did AIT (Advanced Individual Training), I did Jump School, I did Rangers Special Forces School, I did Weapons School, I did Intelligence School, I did NCO School. I was graduated at the top five percent of the class but the idea of war scared me." (This is the only time he speaks of being afraid though he was involved in a good many dangerous actions.) "I ended up getting orders to Vietnam, Special Forces, Green Beret. I didn't chose it. They chose me."

In Vietnam, he was introduced to even more drugs: opium, cocaine, pure heroin, Thai stick. All kinds were available, including alcohol. "Uncle

Sam turned out to be the biggest drug dealer and the biggest liquor dealer in the world. We could get it any time. Ninety-five percent of the people on the base were high at any one time. In a way, I'm glad because when I started losing friends over there, guys who were on my team, it was a way to keep from losing control. I couldn't break down. I was the team leader. But one thing was understood. When we were in the bush, we didn't take any drugs with us, nothing but maybe a few beers. Back on the base you can get high. But out in the bush, no. A lot of guys were getting high in the bush. They were losing their lives. But that was their own fault.

"I was basically in command of our team but I didn't give an order. We planned things together. It was a very unique form of community. A thirteen-man team, going out to do what we did, you have to be very close, very sure of each other. Each guy is trained to act like two, with two different training backgrounds. One guy could be a weapons expert and a medic. Myself, I was weapons and intelligence.

"There were a lot of racial problems in Vietnam, especially with King being assassinated, but not in our team. Our first sergeant was black. Everybody loved him. We didn't look at color. We looked at the individual. There were very few Blacks in the Green Berets but those that were there you could count on. And they had to count on you.

"We were the best of the best, the elite. We were the assassins. We were the guys who were dropped behind enemy lines to do certain things: assassinations, take out weapons, supply depots, things like that. And my base of operations was in the heart of the Ho Chi Min Trail. We were unofficially in Cambodia and Laos before they said we could go.

"Once we were out in the bush for a full ninety days when we lost the first two guys on my team. We put them in body bags and brought them back to be sent home. When we got to the base, we went in, got out our alcohol and our drugs and just sat there. No one talked about it. No one wanted to. No one wanted to break down. But now I feel like, if I had broken down, it would have done a lot of good. But I couldn't. I was the team leader. I have two very functional, artificial kneecaps caused by shrapnel, same day, same battle, plus my hand and my forehead. Our base was overrun. We evacuated everybody and we left. We had no choice. I was hit and didn't realize it. I left Nam on a stretcher. They did a reconstruction on my face.

"I wanted to go back. I requalified myself. I was able to jump, to run, to do what you normally do. But I could never go back because the Vietcong had posters out on certain commands, including mine. My condition doesn't bother me, *per se,* because I don't let it. Only now and then. I know when it's going to rain."

He didn't want to fight anymore but he wanted to stay in the Service. He was put on courier duty to Brussels and other bases in Europe. He did a lot of work with British, French, German and the Israeli Intelligence; learned a lot especially from the Israelis, not only about Intelligence but how to survive. "I also learned that the CIA had money in mind. Vietnam, for instance, is very rich in rubber, some oils and minerals. In fact, all the Intelligence work done by all Intelligence agencies — the KGB, the CIA, British Intelligence — has to do with money.

"I stayed in the Service for twenty-four years. I don't know why I stayed so long. That's why I'm writing a book about it. Maybe I'll find the answer there.

"I'm one hundred percent different from what I was before I joined the military. Now I'm bothered by helicopters flying overhead, fireworks going off, or a thunderstorm like the one we had last night. When the first flash went off, I went under the bed. I thought it was an artillery shell. I still have nightmares constantly about the war; horrendous, outrageous dreams. It's what's referred to as post traumatic stress disorder (PTSD). It used to be called shell shock. It's a way of life for anybody who has been in combat. The nightmares are traumatic, soul-wrenching. They cause frustration, depression, sometimes anger so that you want to strike out one way or another. The only people who know how to handle this are the guys who've been there. They know they have to let the dream run through. Because the nightmares are mostly about the enemy coming at you and when you're woken, your first reaction is to try to kill the first person you see. I still have psychotherapy when I need it. I think the nightmares will end once I finish the book. While I'm writing it, I think they'll intensify.

"Another thing that worries me is I have this uncontrollable hatred for anybody of the Asian race: Korean, Chinese, Thai, Malaysian; men, women or children. I think it began with the first man we lost. He died with a hole in the back of his head, killed by a shot from a grass hut. I carried him back to the chopper and back to the base even though he was dead. There were no tears. There was just a dimple of hate that kept growing and growing inside me for all Oriental people.

"Today, I have a better control of that feeling but I still have these little things. I was offered a supervisory position which would have paid about $40,000 a year. I turned it down because many of their employees are Vietnamese. I would be a risk to them and to myself. Here, at CCSK, we work with some Oriental students as volunteers. I have no hatred for them. I get along fine with them. There's a young Korean lady who's very interested in my book and I've read passages to her. But I still find myself slipping back into the old attitude. I'm worried that maybe one day, when I've had a nightmare, I'll come in here, see some of these Asian people and walk out again. I've done that before because I didn't want to hurt anybody."

But there are two Vietnamese people he longs to see. One is his daughter. "I never saw her grow up, I never saw her take her first step, never heard her talk. Now she's twenty-two — if she's still alive. She's one-third American, one-third French and one-third Vietnamese, so her system's all messed up." Her mother, Claudine, his first wife, is part Vietnamese and part French. She was in danger in Vietnam because her father, a French businessman, was very pro-American. Al went to see them in Saigon whenever he could. He has married again, though according to Vietnamese law, he's still married to Claudine.

"As far as I know, they never made it out of there. I'm beginning to think about them again, more than ever now, because of my book and I start questioning myself about what I've done to get them out. I've written to Claudine's family but I haven't heard anything. I've gone to every Federal agency you can think of. I've even talked to friends who went back to Vietnam but they found nothing. Unfortunately, my dear, sweet government doesn't want to help as much as they said they would. I volunteered to go back but they said no. These thoughts have been haunting me for twenty-three years, since the day I left combat in Vietnam. I wanted her to get out but she insisted on waiting for me. We made plans to go together but the base was totally overrun. 284 died. I could say 285 because I died, too. I'm buried with all those guys.

"My second marriage was a mistake. For a while, it was great. Then my wife got into drugs. We're separated but I still see my family. My youngest son, Neddy, is like me, basically. We're extremely close. In fact, I got off drugs and alcohol because of him. One day, when he was about three years old, he did something any normal three-year-old might do. But I went off the deep end, and screamed and raved like a banshsee. He just stood there shaking and crying and turning white. I dropped to my knees, held him real tight and said, 'Daddy's sorry. Daddy's just sick.' He pulled away and looked at me and said, 'You're not sick, Daddy. I love you.' Those words, boom [claps hands], that was what I needed to get off drugs. Everyone says they need something to get off them. That was my reason. I looked at myself in the full-length mirror and I looked like death. That night I trashed all my drugs. The next morning I woke up and said, 'Oh, wow, I need to get high.' But there was nothing there. Then Neddy's words came back to me and I said, 'That's it. I don't need to get high.' And I started on the road to recovery.

"I've been off drugs and alcohol for four and a half years now but I can go back any time — and kill myself. It's a constant struggle. I haven't had anything since Christmas Eve when I had a glass of white wine. I'm writing instead. It's depressing, it's heart-wrenching, it's soul-tearing but tonight I'm going to write chapter two and I know that after that, I'll be able to relax and then I'll sleep. I'll be up again at 4:00 AM to exercise. Next month I'm going to start running again. And, on the first of April, I'm kicking one more habit — cigarettes. So I can get back into shape. It's something I have to do for myself. Pretty soon, I'm going to put myself in the VA for a few weeks, what we call a clean-up, just to get rid of the anxiety. And then I'll put myself in again for six months for a major overhaul. It's my choice.

"I believe the Vietnam veterans came back more violent than they were before. I'm one hundred percent more violent but I've learned to control it to the best of my ability. We're also deadlier *without* a gun than your average person on the street with a gun. It's the way we were trained. And now, you've got all these kids out there, wanting to play with guns. There should be a federal law saying anyone under seventeen caught with a gun goes to a US military camp. If you're older, you go into the Service for two years. They want to play with guns, give them all the guns they want. But, unfortunately, you can't do that in this country. Because our society is the biggest pansy society on the face of the earth. My little one said, 'Daddy, I want to be in the Service like you.' I said, 'No, I don't want you to be like me. I don't want you in the Service. It's not pretty. It's not like watching Rambo or GI Joe on TV.' You die physically or you die mentally. I've died mentally."

One day, on a New Hope bus, a young Black started to bang on the back of Al's seat. Al told him to "chill it." The boy was going to pull a gun but Al did what is called "dead staring." The boy turned on him and said, "You have the devil in your eyes." "Yes, I know. He's my brother." The boy said, "I'll kill you." By the time he pulled the gun, he would have been dead. "I would have killed him with my bare hands. He would have been splashed all over the back of the bus. And I wouldn't have blinked an eye. [Claps his hands between every few words]

"That's the way Uncle Sam trained us. We were trained in every aspect of killing — with or without a weapon. I can survive any type of situation. That's the one thing Uncle Sam gave me. At times I've been accused of not having feelings. And, at times, they're right. I shut everything down because I still can't handle a lot of pain. People in this country still have this thing that men shouldn't cry. Which is the biggest *malarkey* I ever heard. I'm a man. Just because I cry when something painful hits me, doesn't make me any less of a man.

"I liked my army career. I liked it all: the combat and the physical training because it kept me in shape and fit and active; the Intelligence gathering also kept me active." Yet now he is able to view a good deal of it with objectivity. "I miss it today. I've gained twenty pounds since I got out. I'm going back into training. But I don't want to go back to the Service. Though if a world war broke out right now, I would try to get into it. That's because I have a twenty-one-year-old son who is flying around for the US Air Force."

When Al got out of the Service, he took over his father's business. The business went well and he kept his drinking and drugs away from the office. But the business failed because of the economy and he had a nervous breakdown. "It was a combination of a lot of pressure and PTSD. I just went off the deep-end. I was sleeping with a loaded 9mm gun under my pillow. I still do. It's the conditioning Uncle Sam gives you. Neddy was spending weekends with me and I was having nightmares. I'm thankful that he never came in to try to help me. I might have killed him, killed my own son. Finally I went to the VA. I did a lot of talking about PTSD and it helped. A lot of stuff was still suppressed — about my wife and daughter over there. I never did tell about that.

"I try not to be military with my family. I try to talk to them like a friend. I get money from Uncle Sam but it doesn't come to me. It goes into the bank for my children. It's set up so I can't touch it. No matter how bad things get, it's for them.

"I've been in all three shelters in the city. They're all right, they're not as bad as people make them out to be but you have no privacy. A lot of times I'd take a sleeping bag and go off to be by myself, get my own thoughts going. I've slept in Green Woods in the middle of summer and in the middle of winter, too. I had a GI sleeping bag so I was pretty warm. But life on the streets is not easy. Jefferson House helped a little but, generally, I got along by myself. I got on City Assistance by myself and I found my place by myself. It was tough because landlords don't want to take people on City because the City doesn't pay enough.

"I spent a lot of time looking for a job, getting my face slapped and the door slammed on me. I was looking for anything. I didn't care what it was. After a while I just said, the hell with it. Instead, I got involved with organizations for the homeless. I spoke at demonstrations in New Hope and at the capital and wrote letters to the newspapers. There are a lot of people out there who blame us, the people on the street, for our condition. Three hundred years ago, their ancestors said no one in this state will ever go without food or shelter. If they take away any more, people are going to start killing each other and that's what the successful ones want. They want to be rid of us." (This is a sentiment expressed by many of the homeless.) "But they can't be sure we won't go for them. I will. I'll lead the way. I voted for Richard Nixon. After Nixon, I turned my back on politicians. But I'm not through with politics. I'm still fighting for people."

He got involved with the soup kitchen because he uses it. He enjoys the cooking which he performs with vigor and pride and enthusiasm. "A bachelor has to learn to cook. There are books in the library on feeding one hundred people and more. They're standard, easy recipes. But now I have to write my book and get my business started." It is an agency, primarily, for finding lost children and missing people for which he hopes to get a grant or loan from The Small Business Administration. "I've had experience. I've searched for plenty of people — and I've destroyed plenty of people.

"Sometimes I seriously think about going back to Vietnam to find my wife and my daughter, and to stay. But the Vietcong government still wants to get their hands on certain people like the Special Forces, to try them for war crimes. We did a lot of underhanded things, I admit that.

"I don't need America, America needs me. When I was a courier, I got out into the countryside in many different countries and met the people. They were warm and friendly. They'd invite you in, feed you, get you drunk. It's a different way of life, totally relaxed. It gave me a lot of perspective on life in the States. We're too fast-paced, always rushing off, going nowhere fast. We're just too geared up, trying to speed ahead of everybody else, trying to be number one. I don't have a favorite country. They're all my favorite. I might even go to Russia."

RAY

"If I don't get a job and the cuts go through,
I'll be be back on drink and drugs and robberies again.
And that will be the end for me."

He speaks with a rapid-fire delivery as if he had thought it all out before. Independent in thought and sometimes ruthless, he can also be humane as is his attitude toward the Vietnamese people and the Blacks in the American Army. A natural leader, he is active, along with his girlfriend, Josie, in PEOPLE FIRST.

I began in a cold-water flat in New Hope with the toilet in the hall and a bathtub that was pulled out from under the kitchen sink on Saturday night. I was the youngest child. Everything belonged to my brother before it belonged to me so nothing ever fit. My father, my mother's second husband, left us for another woman when I was six. My mother was out working all the time. She didn't bring me up. I brought myself up."

She married her third husband when Ray was about nine. "I hated him.

He had grown kids of his own and he didn't really want somebody else's kids. He had plenty of money. He took care of my mother, but not us kids. We weren't his kids."

The family moved to a small town outside New Hope and, for Ray, that meant fist fights every day. "It wasn't about race. It was about me, because I was an outsider. 'You don't belong here. Get out. Get lost. You're this, you're that. Your mother's a…' I had to fight all the time. Eventually they got tired of it."

The family was Catholic so when Ray was kicked out of public school — "I hung out with the wrong people" — he was sent to parochial school. He hated it, hated the religious teaching. "I didn't really think that belonged in the classroom. There's church and there's school. If you want to go to church, go to church. The only thing I liked about parochial school was that the actual school work was challenging, as opposed to public school where you don't learn much. I really liked math." The teachers were all nuns and very strict. They whacked Ray's palms constantly with rulers for not paying attention. He dropped out when he was sixteen. "Unfortunately," he says now.

"Home wasn't comfortable. It wasn't my home. It was my mother's. You live in her house, you live by her rules. Girlfriends? 'You can have all the girlfriends you want. But you're not bringing them home. Get a motel room. I'm not running a whore house.'"

He joined the army at seventeen during the Vietnam War — to get away. There was no one to warn him against it. His mother signed for him. "Maybe this'll straighten you out," she said. He was in the Airborne Division.

Once overseas, he realized that only about ten percent of the population, those with money, wanted us there. "The poor people were being bled by their 'democratic' government. After we got there everybody, I think, had some kind of awakening. Unless they were sociopaths and just wanted to kill people."

In Cameron Bay, the natives were entirely dependent on US dollars so the army was treated well. But as Ray got farther along, he saw that the poverty of the people was increased by the war. And he saw the defoliation. "I don't blame these people for being bitter. If foreigners came into my homeland and destroyed my crops and shot up my home and it wasn't safe to go out even in daylight, I'd want to stop them, too.

"During the day you'd see saw the Vietnamese working for the army: cooking, cleaning, laundering. But at midnight, they'd come back, hordes of them in black pajamas, and attack. When the shooting was over, they dragged their dead away. The next morning, everything was back to normal.

"The Tet offensive was the worst I ever saw. I couldn't even estimate how many people were killed, Vietnamese mostly. Some of them didn't even have weapons, just machetes and sticks. They were shot down before they even hit the perimeter. I was in a ditch — in the perimeter."

The Airborne was stationed right up front with sandbags in bunkers instead of barracks. He was wounded twice. The first time, he had twenty-one stitches in his forehead and, after two weeks, he was sent back to his unit. The second time a piece of bomb fragment shattered his elbow. They gave him a choice: go back or go home. He went back. "I had friends there. I didn't want to just leave them. I had to sign a waiver that the Army wouldn't be responsible."

The companies were integrated. "There were more Blacks than Whites though it wasn't their war and they knew it. These lads were abused before they went into the Service, abused while they were in the Service, and they weren't going to take any more abuse. Not over there. Over there, they were top dog." They kept to themselves: Blacks stayed with Blacks, Whites stayed with Whites. Some Whites wanted to join them but they wouldn't allow it. "Go back to your crappy friends. You don't want to be hanging out with niggers. You don't hang out with niggers at home. Why you want to hang out with them here?"

One day, Ray decided to try to cross over. "I'm used to being around black people. It doesn't make any difference to me. 'We've all gotta be here,' I told them. 'Why can't we get along?' 'You get along with your own people,' they said." But in the end they let him stay because he could play the guitar and the harmonica and could play rock music.

"We didn't have a drug problem in Vietnam. We had plenty of drugs. They caught guys with footlockers full of marijuana. They weren't selling it. It was so cheap, they were giving it away. I used drugs before I went to Vietnam but I wasn't really addicted. Take it or leave it. But in Vietnam, I stayed high all the time. Everybody did. We didn't function, not really. It was dangerous but when you're high, you don't care. Officers were using it, too. I've seen some some pretty high COs on duty—lieutenants and captains. I'm sure that more than one helicopter crashed because the pilot was high on dope. People were punished for it but there wasn't much more punishment they could give you. Just being there was punishment."

One night Ray was sent out with a group on a "listening post." They were supposed to camp out all night, watching a trail and listening for movements. Instead, "A couple of bags of dope up the nose and everyone slept."

"Friendly fire" was fairly common. "If you had a sergeant or a second lieutenant or a captain who was going to get you killed in the field, you killed him first. It wasn't accidental."

He spent three years in the army; twelve months in actual combat. "I grew up five years in twelve months."

He came back and ran into Peaceniks. "I thought the only reason people were draft dodgers was because they were scared. I didn't even know what a pacifist was. I hadn't finished high school. I was twenty. A boy threw a rotten melon at me as I got off the bus in New Hope. I must have beat him half to death. The cops came and arrested *him.* I was in uniform. Then I went home and proceeded to ruin my life."

He had nightmares. "Everyone made a big thing about the My Lai massacre but there were My Lais everywhere." Once, he had been ordered to kill anything that moved. What moved were women and children and some wounded soldiers. In his dream, they kept running toward him with their hands out while he kept firing into those open arms. He dreamed about a Vietcong stronghold which they bombed continuously for twenty-four hours a day. Hundreds of civilians were killed. Finally, after two weeks, they were sent in, thinking it was all clear. But, suddenly, Viet Cong soldiers came popping up out of the ground all over the place. Ray got through. A couple of his close friends did not.

He even had daymares. Once, driving down Main Street in the middle of the afternoon, a car back-fired. He jumped out of his pick-up truck and ran.

He had other problems. He married a girl he had known before the war but he had a hard time getting on with anyone else. "Before the war, I hung out with a lot of people. After the war, I kinda went into hiding. My behavior pattern deteriorated. My friends became less and less acceptable. Because *I* was less and less acceptable. I was using alcohol, I was using drugs. I didn't want to know people. I didn't want to talk to anyone but my wife. I began to collect animals: horses, dogs, cats, chickens, a goat. I spent my time with them. And I always carried a gun. Ever since Vietnam.

"I took money from anyone. I didn't care. Talk green. That was my attitude. Before the war, if I could see a way to make an easy buck, I made it. But I wouldn't go out of my way. I didn't look for it. But when I came home, I was scanning everything to see if I could make money out of it. My brother was in the war before I was. He came out crazy."

Ray got a job in construction and he had the GI Bill. He was making money, even saving money. And he was doing a little business on the side in stolen goods. "I did it because I was greedy. I didn't really need more money. I just wanted more money. I wasn't stealing it myself, just moving it for friends that worked on the railroad, stuff they took off freight cars: TV sets, stereos, refrigerators, freezers. They paid me to get rid of it. I had to build a garage on the house to store it in. That's the first thing I ever built, a two-car garage." He even became involved in drug-dealing.

One night he had a fight with a drug dealer who owed him $75,000 for cocaine. They were alone in a deserted parking lot when the dealer pulled a gun and announced he wasn't going to pay. "I knew he was about to shoot me, so I pulled a gun, too. And I fired first. He died the next day. They gave me ten to twenty years for second-degree manslaughter. They didn't like me."

He went on taking drugs in prison — and alcohol — but he kept it under control. Everyone who took drugs or alcohol outside went right on using them inside. "You could get anything you wanted in prison — if you could afford it. The guards sell it to the prisoners and the prisoners sell it to each other. Prisoners have money from deals they make or from the Hobby Shop."

Prisoners could go to the Hobby Shop instead of to Recreation. They had to pay for their materials but the tools were provided. There were no longer enough real jobs in the prison for everyone and most prisoners preferred to work rather than sit around all day doing nothing. Ray was certainly one of those for he signed up for several different programs.

Prisoners could sell what they made — to visitors or guards or through the prison store — and the money went right into their account; or they could send it home. Ray made lots of furniture which sold well, especially small bars. He also worked in the upholstery shop, in the furniture factory, and took a small appliance repair course where they fixed small appliances that were donated because they weren't really worth fixing. The manufacturers got a tax write-off. Ray sold some of the appliances he repaired to the guards — under the table.

"Books? I could get almost any book I wanted. You could go to the library whenever it was open during Recreation. If I couldn't get it at the prison library, I could probably get it at a discount. A lot of companies offered discounts to inmates. I read a lot: Stephen King, Ray Bradbury. I read a lot."

One week there was a rumor that there would be a big altercation between the Blacks and the Puerto Ricans during a baseball game. "I thought it would be a good fight so I brought some popcorn with me and a big jar of Kool Aid. Spectator sport stuff, you know. Like the gladiators."

Suddenly he saw the guards putting baseball bats out on the field. "There must have been thirty bats out there. Then the visiting team from Wellington Prison arrived and the recreation supervisor put out every baseball bat *he* could find. There were bats all over the yard and it wasn't the inmates that put them there. It was the *staff*. The Administration expected it to be a racial conflict between Blacks and Puerto Ricans and they had more guards than prisoners out there. But suddenly the prisoners began picking up baseball bats. Soon there were white guys with baseball bats, black guys with baseball bats, Puerto Rican guys with baseball bats. But they weren't fighting each other. They were fighting the guards!

"What provoked it was the treatment. They put all the new guards on the 4:00 to 12:00 shift. Because they're new, they're probably scared to death so they put on this tough guy, John Wayne attitude. It made people mad. They treated all the prisoners that way. So now there were white guys with baseball bats, black guys with baseball bats, Puerto Rican guys with baseball bats — and guards lying around all over the ground. A lieutenant had locked the gate so the prisoners couldn't get back to their cells and the guards couldn't get out either.

"The whole prison was locked out for two weeks. No showers, no commissary, no mail. We ate in shifts. It took four feedings to do one cell block so they were feeding us twenty-four hours a day. Breakfast might be at 11:00 in the morning, lunch at 3:00 in the afternoon and dinner at 10:00 at night. There was running water in the cells but it was difficult to wash your hair in the sink. Especially as we had to push buttons to make the water run—one for hot, one for cold."

Ray served only seven of his ten-to-twenty year sentence. "I had a good lawyer and I had a good parole program set up for myself: a wife, a kid, a home, a job. My boss told me he would take me back. He was on my visiting list. Also, I went to the shrink. He didn't help. It was just a game I had to play to get parole."

Out of prison, Ray thought he had totally lost his mind. He didn't tell anyone but he felt as if he'd been in a coma for seven years. Things had changed radically while he was gone. Buildings had grown taller, streets wider, shops had disappeared. People looked older, some even degenerate. He had changed, too, but didn't realize it. "I was a lot tougher than when I went in. I wasn't as willing to bend to other people's will. If I believed something in my own mind, nobody could tell me anything different. I was very bitter. Very resentful.

"Not everyone reacts to prison in the same way. There's a few people who come out and turn their whole life around — for the better. But — I hate to say it, I really hate to say it — the majority of the people who go to prison once will go to prison again. Because there's no incentive to get better there — just bitter. People who commit crimes have a reason for it. I'm not saying that's always the case. There are some who just enjoy ruining other people. But most of them commit a crime for a reason. Usually, it's because of financial need. And when they get out of prison, the reason is still there. Only worse. Because after prison, it's even harder to find a job."

When Ray got home, he went through a good many jobs, looking for what he wanted to do. There were lots of jobs. He didn't want to go back to construction. He worked in a machine shop, a box shop and, finally, a rubber mill which was a haven for alcoholics. "The owner was an active alcoholic, the foreman was an active alcoholic and all the mill men were alcoholics. I found out why. There was a lot of pressure and heat on the job and if you ever got your hand caught between the rollers of their machines and couldn't hit the safety bar in time, your whole arm would go with it. It was a kind of obscene job, too, because we were making mortuary rubber for undergarments and sheeting. They use rubber so you can't smell the embalming. Soon I was an alcoholic, too.

"When I left, I stopped drinking for a while. I can just stop, on and off. Which makes it dangerous because nobody knows when I'm going to start again. It happens when I'm bored or unhappy but most of all, it's because I want to drink. After a while, I get tired of it. I get disgusted with myself and I stop."

It was summer when he quit his job. He stayed home and did a lot of property improvement: put up new fences, did farm work, put a new roof on the house, put in a new driveway and a basketball court. "If I had a choice, that's the way I would like to spend my time, doing a lot of different things. But that wasn't making any money. Fortunately, my wife was working full-time. She'd been working in the same place for years. She ran a knitting machine.

"I looked for work in a half-assed way. Jobs were getting scarcer and that seven year gap in my work record didn't help. The wife was sick of me hanging around the house and I was sick of being nagged at. I decided the best thing I could do for both of us was to pack up and get out."

He lived in his pickup truck for a while — wherever he could park it outside the city: in Marion, in Watford, in Parkside. He still had a little money. Finally, he came to New Hope looking for work. But now, there wasn't any. His money was running out, he wasn't on Welfare and it was getting too cold to sleep in the truck.

One night he wandered into the soup kitchen and got more than a cup of soup. For one thing, he met his girlfriend, Josie. She wasn't on Welfare either. She was living in a dump and about to be evicted. He stayed with her for a couple of weeks and, finally, they were both on Welfare. "Now we have a room on Westwood Avenue. It's good. I like it. Things are just beginning to fall into place for us. But if these Welfare cuts go through, we'll lose it all.

"Something else I got at the soup kitchen was a political education. I never had any real interest in politics. Now I do. It started last year when the legislature wanted to cut Welfare so we started political action in the shelters and the soup kitchens.

"We had our first meeting in the soup kitchen and organized PEOPLE FIRST. We don't have any officers. We have weekly meetings with an agenda. Sometimes co-dependency works. And we really are co-dependent.

"Any time you see me in a jacket and tie, you know I've either been at a job interview or at the State House, testifying at a committee hearing.

I testify a lot and I help get out flyers.

"On Clean-Up Day in May, we're going to find the worst place in town and we're going in there and get dirty, real dirty, and clean it up. And that has nothing to do with Welfare reform. It has to do with people saying, 'These people are all lazy and don't want to work.' We have an idea for a worker-owner temporary labor company and a trash pick-up company and we want to start some Service for youth in the community. Because, God knows, these kids need some positive role models besides people standing on street corners selling cocaine.

"I'm clean now and I hope to stay that way. And I'm hoping to get a job, through a friend of mine, doing maintenance work. But if I don't get a job and the cuts go through, I'll be back on drink and drugs and robberies again. And that will the end for me."

THE SKILLED

"...they support the fabric of the world,
And their prayer is the practice of their trade."
— *Ecclesiasticus 38:33–34*

Lonnie (welder)
Gordon (furrier)
Morgan (railroad)

These men, with their skills cooped up inside them, feel their deprivation keenly. They have been stripped, not only of their livelihood, but also of their self-respect and, to a certain extent, their identity — for we are, in part, what we do. But most of all perhaps, they have been deprived of the pleasure of exercising their hard-earned expertise.

Each takes pride and pleasure in his special competence. Curtis, an electrical engineer, likes messing around with electricity. The railroad is Morgan's first love. Tyler enjoys manipulating heavy machinery — "That's what I really like to do." And Lonnie is proud that "Anything that needs to be weld, I can weld it."

Only Gordon, the furrier, lost his job through lapses of his own and blames himself bitterly. Actually, the job bored him. It was not his choice but his father's and he had accepted it for all the wrong reasons. He realized, too late, that he really wanted to be a pharmacist but his unforgiving father made that impossible. He was left with no money, no job, no home and a heavy burden of guilt.

Though proud of their skills, these men are all willing and able to turn their hands to any job they can find: cooking, dishwashing, carpentry, construction, electrical work, warehouse work, office work and other far less skilled jobs. But now there are no jobs at all. They are stuck in the soup kitchens where only their bodies are fed.

LONNIE

"I like welding.
That's what I been trained to do."

He is a good-looking African American with a strong southern accent and all his teeth. In spite of his jaunty red cap and red jacket, he has a shy, quiet manner. His love for his grandparents, impressively demonstrated, is touching and rare in my samples. He comes to the kitchen alone and leaves alone. He's thirty-two but looks much younger.

My grandparents raised me from an infant. They were the only parents I knew till I got about thirteen. Then they tell me who my real mother is. She had me when she was in high school. She'd come an visit so I know her but not as my mother. The only mother I know was my grandmother. After I get old to understand things, then they tell me that she was my mother. I was surprised an, in a way, hurt. As a kid, you know, but after I get older, then I learned to accept it." This is the only time he mentions her. "I did never get a chance to know my father. Only father I know is my grandfather.

"I was raised up along with my uncles, my mother's brothers. The youngest one, he's about five years older than me. My grandparents raised up my two sisters and my two brothers also. We had the same mother but different fathers."

Lonnie grew up in a very small town in South Carolina. While he was still at school, he helped his grandmother run the family farm. "We was raising pigs, chickens, plant cukes, mostly corn for the pigs and the chickens, garden peas, squash for the house. My uncles had finished school. The oldest had already left. I was right behind the youngest who was five years older than me. When he went, it was just me. I was about twelve when he left an I took up the farm work where he left off. It wasn't that hard because I already knew what to do.

"I was kinda bad, selfish, but I never did steal. I had money cause I used to work for money. I worked for the next door neighbor, a white guy, after school. He had a big farm an he payin like six, seven dollars a hour. So, end of the week, I had money. My grandmother didn't take it. She always said, 'If you want anything, work for it. What you work for is yours.' I was real close to my grandmother.

"I'd go out, stay out late. Get drunk. Guys of my age, four or five get together an we'd go an party with guys that were older than us. They had cars. They'd take us to different clubs and we used to lie on our age. My grandparents didn't know about that. Only thing they knew about was me stayin out late an they didn't approve about that too much." (This is a theme that runs through his story but it is hard to connect the wild, party-loving young man he describes with the rather gentle, soft-spoken guest I see.)

"I was raised in church. Methodist. My grandparents, they go to church every Sunday. As a kid, as we were comin up, me and my sisters, we had to go to church along with them. We didn't have no choice. After a certain age, I used to hide my shoes where I would be late and not have to go. When I was over twelve, my grandmother said, 'You old enough now to know right from wrong. If you don't want to go, you don't have to.' But my grandmother an my grandfather, they was very strictly church. When I got out of the Service, I started going to church for a while. Then I just broke off.

"I quit school when I was fifteen because of racial problems. The school had just integrated. We used to fight every day, three or four times a day. But that wasn't why I quit. I got kicked out for fighting. White boys got kicked out. Principal kicked everybody out. I didn't get kicked out permanently, only for two weeks. But I didn't went back. I was frustrated. I was mad. So I quit.

"My grandfather was rough. He said, 'Well, if you don't want to go to school, you have to get a job.' I was lookin for a job but at that age ain't nobody gonna hire me. An my grandfather, he was no help. He put pressure on me, hopin that I would go back to school."

Lonnie heard about Job Corps through a friend. It was an on-the-job training program for young people who had left school and wanted to further their education and learn a trade. They had school for half a day and worked at the trade of their choice the other half. Everything was paid for: lodging, three meals a day, vouchers for clothes, plus $15 a week.

There was no Job Corps in South Carolina so Lonnie went to Louisville, Kentucky. It was his first time away from home. "I didn't really know what I was getting into. But I went for it. Me and my friend. He was a home boy. I knew him from school, growing up."

The dormitories were racially mixed: Black, White and Mexican and divided into sections. Each section had a section leader and a dorm leader.

Lonnie made dorm leader. "They have a TV room an a library. You want to read, you go to the library. You want to look at TV, you go to the TV room. Each dorm have a security guard. Keep you from fighting. Because in the TV room you want to look at Channel 4, another person want to look at another channel, so that would be a problem. So what we do, we used to flip coins or pull match sticks for whatever show we want to look at that night. We had a lotta fights over other things, too. Over people stealing clothes, broke into your locker. Wasn't too much fightin over racial problems. The real problem was if you're gay. Then you stay in your own group and if you're not, you stay in your own group. If they found out you're gay, they sent you to another camp where the majority is gay.

"What I did, I took up welding. I finished the program. I was there thirteen months. There was a place in South Dakota would have given me a job but I was too young. They wouldn't put insurance on me because I was still a minor.

"So what I did, I asked my grandmother an grandfather to sign me for the military. The people at the Center, they didn't want me to leave. They said I was a good kid. They wanted me to stay and take up another trade. Which I wish I had done. I don't know why I didn't. I wasn't tired of school. I was tired of that Center. I was ready to get away from that. Get out, get some fresh air. I got my welding certificate. Any job come up in welding, I can probably get it. They wanted me to take up carpentry or brick masonry but that would mean another thirteen, fourteen months. So I write my grandparents an beg them to sign me for the military. My grandmother, she called me at the Center and asked me, 'Are you sure?' I said, 'I'm sure.' She said, 'Are you very sure?' She didn't want to sign for me but I kept naggin an nagging an naggin an naggin. Then, finally, she signed the paper. I went to Paris Island. To the Marines."

He was in the Marines for four years. It was the Marines because he scored low on his tests and the Marines got all the lowest scorers. He didn't get into his chosen field, either. They put him into field artillery. "Know what I was doing? I was goin round blowin things up. I would blow up trees, blow up bunkers, blow up tanks, you know? Just for practice.

"I write my grandmother to sign me out. But she wouldn't because she said that's what I wanted. First two weeks was tough. They make you run everywhere you're going. Even to the bathroom. From the time you get up, you run. You do that for the first three weeks. After that you go to school, technical school. They learn you about the different types of weapons. Learn you how to mix up some gas to burn people up. I'm serious. What I'm talking about is napalm. Learn you how to defend yourself in combat situation. After that a lot of runnin, a lot of exercise. You be in very good shape.

"Paris Island's in South Carolina. Very hot. The quarters were very comfortable, very clean. Man, you could eat off the floor. Clean sheet every day. God Almighty, you scrub the place down two times a day. 4:00 o'clock in the mornin, they wake you up to do that. Every day. Sometime it may be 3:00 o'clock. That's military trainin. First six weeks is mainly physical and mental trainin. To see how you can take it. They make you mad, insult you, scream at you, hit you, make you fight. If you wanna fight someone, that's okay. That's good. Any time a fight come up, they like that. What they do, they make a circle, an let you fight, get it off your chest. They don't do that anymore.

"But after the first six weeks, mostly you go to class, learnin different types of weapons, look at war films, learn about tanks. The other men were just as terrified as I was. They was very mixed. White, Black, Mexican, Puerto Rican. Officers an NCO were mixed. No racial problems. In military, you don't have to worry about racial problems too much. Because when that come up, they kick you out with a bad discharge. But you gotta get caught. You can't tell by their color how people'll treat you. Some mean, some not.

"When I first got in, I got into trouble a few times. Didn't follow orders, got caught sleeping on duty, stay out too late, partyin. That was my biggest problem. I liked to go out an party. Now, how can I stand watch if I'm half drunk and sleepy? Boot camp was twelve weeks back then. After that I graduated, dressed up in a green uniform. The grandparents didn't come. Grandma had to take care of the farm. Grandfather had to go to work.

"I went to the Philippines. It's not safe out there. Walkin the street's not safe. You could get killed or shot. Lots of pretty girls in the Philippines. Made sergeant there — lost it. Never even sewed my stripes on. I was AWOL. Left the base and don't come back for two or three days. It was adventure. We wanted to see the whole island. It was beautiful. Reminded me of the farm in a way. They had corn fields. I didn't know they grew corn like that. We had drinkin parties. So we got busted. On a base like that, everybody got busted one time or another. Every night there was a party. Only had a short time to go, so I didn't really care. No drugs. You could have all the liquor you want, they don't care. But no drugs. You even mention drugs, they lock you up and forget you. I smoked reefers, nothing stronger than marijuana, but I was very careful. I didn't get addicted. Still performed my duties. I could have signed up for another four years and pick up sergeant again. But I didn't know what I wanted to do so I thought it best I get out.

"I stayed home for about a year. I got a job paintin just for a couple of weeks. I was lookin for a welding job but they wasn't hirin. And the area I was livin in, you needed transportation. All the jobs were way out.

"I started gettin into trouble with the cops, drivin without a license, little minor things like that. My grandad told me, he said 'Job can't find you, you gotta find it.' So I came to New Hope because I had a uncle here. I stayed with him. He's a chemist, workin at Upjohn. I stayed with him about three, four months till I got myself situated. Then I got a job with Carson's. They build steel basement jobs. I was a welder. Started me off with $6.00 an hour and worked up to $10 in no time. I stayed there about six years. That was good. I liked the job. I like welding. That's what I been trained to do. An I got good benefits. I had a car, a nice apartment.

"Until my grandfather got a stroke. My grandmother, she was doing all the work an takin care of him. I just couldn't let her do all that by herself. So I quit Carson's and I went down there to help her take care of him. Before I quit, I tried to get a leave of absence but they said they couldn't give it to me but if I came back they could rehire me. I'd have to start all over again but I said, 'That sounds good.' I wasn't thinkin about a job then. I was just thinkin bout gettin down there an helpin my grandfather an my grandmother. The rest of the family was all up north an everybody in the family was for hisself. Nobody would make that move, that sacrifice. My uncles, my two sisters and my two brothers, they didn't make a move. They told my grandmother to pop him in a home and that would be less work for her. But after bein married for fifty years, she didn't want to hear that. She wasn't goin for that. I wanted to let her have her way so I moved down there to help her.

"While I was there, I got a job as a welder, making CP boats and I was takin care of Grandad. Until my grandmother had a heart attack. I called my aunt because I didn't know what to do. So everybody came down and that's when my aunt told my grandmother they would take care of her and put my grandfather in a home. And I say, 'Well, time for me to come back this way and look for a job.' I should have stayed up here. I liked my job up here. The boat job was all right, too, but I got laid off from that. They were tryin to bring in a union and the owner got mad. He didn't want no union so he laid off the last twelve people that just got hired. I was one of them. Union never did get in.

"I come back up here tryin to get my job back at Carson's. But the guy that hired me, he got a transfer to Arkansas and I can't get in touch with him. So I say, 'Oh, man, that knocks me off.' I stayed with my uncle. I was on Welfare till I got a part-time job with a recyclin company. I jus keep buggin them till I got on a regular full-time. Sometime I do night work, then they pay more.

"I got my own place now with this old guy. He only need two rooms so I can use the whole apartment. It's on Marshall Avenue, not too far out. He know my people. He know my uncle and them for years. He just like friends. He charge $75 a week. Not much time or money for partying now. Got more relatives than friends here. They're around my age. We get together. I got some relatives in New York and sometimes we go there to party, have a good time.

"I'm a certified welder but, you know, with the cut in Defense, it's tough. I took a test for work on a electric boat. I learned that in Job Corps. Passed the test but a new firm came in and plus the cut-back in defense, they're not hirin. Civilian firms not hirin either. Anything that need to be weld, I can weld. But the problem is, they ain't hirin nobody to make it cause they can't sell it.

"I think I'll stick with the recyclin. With the computer takin over, I'll have no problem. Now everybody want to deal with stuff they can recycle stead of storin and storin till they cumulate so much they don't have no place to live. It's a new company an I think they're gonna expand. So I think I'll stick with them.

"I heard about the soup kitchen from a friend before I started workin. I told him I didn't have no money and he say, 'Man, see all those people on line?' I say, 'Yeah, what they gonna do?' He say, 'Man, they're gonna EAT.' That's how I find out. I can cook. Grandma learned me how to cook. I had to cook for my brothers and sisters. I can bake. I'm a good cook. I like cookin. But you know, if I start to cook, my rent goin up to $85 a week. 'Because,' the old guy say, 'you're usin gas.'

"Plenty of time, I say, thank God they got a soup kitchen. Because, if not, it would be real bad. But I look at it like this: you gotta lotta people come there and they throw away more actually than they eat. That's not human, that's not nice. Lotta people come by an abuse it. A lotta people say I don't want this or that. Ain't nobody forcin you to go there. If anything, they should say, thank God they gotta place to eat if they're hungry. If you're not hungry, don't go there. An you got some people come there an they got money for their partying and they still come there. That's no good. I can't see that. Little thing, like when you get through eatin, throw your plate, your napkin in the garbage can. Some people leavin it right there. They treat their kitchen like that, imagine what their home look like. Basic thing, like you got people come in there try to steal everything their hand can get on. Go out, sell it, just to buy a drug. People come to the kitchen, they have clothes there, some people don't want it for theirselves. They take it out and sell it to buy drugs. That's no good. I would say 75% on drugs. But it don't make everybody act wild.

"I have no complaint about the food. Thank God for it. I come because I ain't got no money. I come an eat an get out. Sometime you try to start a conversation an you get into trouble. If someone start to talk to me, I say something back, but I just like to eat an get out of that atmosphere. Because, you know, seem like everybody got pressure an sometime they gotta take it out on somebody and you never know when they might snap. So, I just try to be out of the way. I don't like crowds. Friends ain't like the way they used to be. When I was in the military, I used to have friends but I don't have friends anymore. So-called friends, they stab you in the back. You really can't trust nobody. But there's a few out there you can trust.

"Right now, I don't even get to party like I used to. But then, I'm gettin a little older and wiser now. Sometime, if I have a little money, I go to the club. Sometime I go with my cousin to the Cardinal's. It's a bar, dancing and that. Go there sometime, sit there, have a few beers.

"I'd like to get my life back the way it was when I was at Carson's. Work five days a week, half day on Saturday, come home, relax, take a shower, cook me a nice meal, go out to the Elks Club. They got a nice group, some respectable people comin there. We have a nice time.

"My grandmother died last week. But my grandfather's still alive, still in a home. He had a stroke from his brain to his feet. On his left side. He can't use that left side. Only thing he can use is his right side. He know what's going on. I saw him at my grandmother's funeral. He say when was I comin back to see him. I say well, hopefully, in about six months. So, hopefully, I can get back to see him. Me and him kinda tight. You know, close. I kinda close to both my grandparents."

GORDON

"Right now, I don't know if I'll ever be able to go home again."

He is a very personable African American, intelligent, decent, well-mannered and well-spoken with a pleasant smile. But in repose, his expression is sad. He dresses neatly in a black jacket and cap and comes with Rowetha, his girlfriend, an African American with a disdainful expression. He is from a rather middle-class background and considers that he was privileged, which makes his present condition especially painful for he believes that he is entirely to blame for his misfortunes. His remorse, his disgust with himself, gives his story a particularly poignant note.

I'm thirty-six but I feel like my life ended when I was twenty-six. I made three bad mistakes in my life. I grew up really privileged, maybe over-privileged. I always felt above most of my friends. I always had it a little better. My father was a fur processor. He just retired after thirty-two years. My mother's an interior decorator. I was the only child. We lived in a nice neighborhood in Brooklyn, the Oceanhill-Brownsville section. It was racially mixed. We had Germans, Italians, Blacks. There was no racial trouble. I got along with everybody. I was pretty versatile."

He went to Catholic schools that were racially mixed, too. "There wasn't any real racism there either. I never worried at all about race. The teachers were nuns and they were very strict. You got bopped on the hand or the behind with a ruler or a paddle for bothering the girls or writing answers on your arm for tests, or just saying something. The Sisters would sneak around and hear you say things and then they'd say, 'Come here,' and you knew you were going to get it. I took my share of that. We had the highest suicide rate in the city.

"At that time, it was accepted that children should take a beating if they did something wrong. I didn't question it. I didn't know anything about what life was like. I just went to school and came home, went to school and came home. I didn't have to work after school like some kids. My father didn't really care about slapping me. Matter of fact, I don't think he came to my room after, maybe, the 8th grade. Never. I'd see him in the kitchen or the dining room or something like that. We were close but in a strange type of way. He acknowledged me as his son and I acknowledged him as a father. I love him and I'm sure he loves me. I guess it has a lot to do with the way he was raised. It's hard for him to express anything like love. I know that he was a good provider. He kept a good roof over our heads.

"My mother was strict. She was more affectionate but she was also the one who disciplined me. My father never hit me. My mother did. She would lay it on me if I did something wrong. But she was also the type of person that would always talk to you about it first. After a couple of mistakes, she'd get fed up. She couldn't see any other way. And then she'd feel so bad. I really felt like I was punishing her when I did something wrong so I tried to walk a pretty straight line.

"I was a really sheltered human being. At home, it was always: come in, lock the door, wait for my mother and father to come home. And then, when I was a little older, I could sit out on the steps but stay inside the gate until my mother came home. So I was like a watchdog for the house."

After high school, he went to New York University to study pharmacy but dropped out after a year. "I think not going away to school was a mistake. I think not living on campus was a mistake. Because I was coming home every night to the same surroundings and seeing the same friends. I had a lot of good friends in my neighborhood. Friendship was like real friendship then. Not like friendship today. But none of my friends followed me to college, none of them were trying to pursue what I was trying to pursue. They could have gone to college. There were programs that would have paid for them. Instead *I* dropped out. That was my first big mistake.

"I dropped out because of a good friend, Calvin. We were like brothers. He went into the Service and I went with him. I joined to get away from my parents and also because I was bored with school. We went in on a 'buddy' program. That is, when you enter the Service with someone from your neighborhood, a person you grew up with, the Service keeps you together. It's guaranteed in your contract.

"I went into the Marine Corps. At that time the Marine Corps was very special, not what it is today. I always picked challenging things. I always wanted to do something that a lot of people didn't do. This was during the Vietnam War. I went in expecting to go to Vietnam. I could have gone to Officers' School. I turned that down because Calvin couldn't cut it and I didn't want to leave him. So I went into the enlisted ranks."

He stayed in for four years and left as a sergeant. He was a fuel analyst which required a high IQ to get in and school for six months. He graduated second in a class of forty-eight. He was sensitive to racism in the Service. "In the mess hall, all the Whites sat together and all the Blacks sat together. In school, you just took the first empty chair."

After school, he was sent to Hanoi and worked a fuel line for jets and fighters "and everything else that moved. I was never actually in combat but it came so close I could hear it. A lot of times we'd get a lot of artillery shells shot at us. It was very dangerous because we slept right inside that field, right beside the stuff. It was like a little city. We were bombed. Once, the enemy was about one-tenth of a mile away from us before they were intercepted. We had hiding places, something like bunkers. I did nine months there. For the first eight months, I hardly slept at all because you'd see bodies going by every day. I was like a walking skeleton.

"At that time, I didn't really know what drugs were like. I grew up on a drug-free block. If you did anything bad, you didn't do it on our block and you didn't do it in our neighborhood. I didn't start taking drugs in the Service, though I saw a lot of it while I was there, especially overseas. Guys would do it right in the barracks at night. But, at that time, drugs were like the farthest thing from my mind. I started drinking beer in the Service but I didn't acquire a taste for alcohol till quite a few years later. Alcohol was never a problem."

His next post was in Camp Lejeune, North Carolina. He was bored and felt he was stagnating. He went through a lot of soul-searching, thinking about his release and what he was going to do with the rest of his life. Would he be able to deal with living at home? "I'm a grown guy now. I'm drinking vodka. I can't be told when to come in at night. When I went home on the weekends, something would tell me, 'Gordon, I don't think living at home would be a good idea.' And believe it or not, I've been home for quite a few visits since I was discharged from the Service but I've never been home to stay.

"The Service changed me a lot. I used to be the type of person that would listen to criticism, take it very easily. But after I came out, I think I lost respect for my father. The things I would say to him. I suppose it was just life, growing up, knowing that I'd been away from home and on my own and I didn't have to listen to this. I often think about that. I respected my officers. I never had any problem with my officers. I was buddies with them. I didn't even have to call them 'Sir' off duty. I was good at taking orders. I had no problem. I picked up rank. I never had any trouble with the men under me, Blacks or Whites, or the one or two Hispanics in the company. I got a very nice discharge."

At home, his father got him a good job in the fur trade with very high pay. "It's a closed thing. It's like three people in the whole city of New York own all the secrets, handed down from the Greeks. They're mostly native Italians and a couple of Jewish guys. It's a father and son thing. They take a son in when there's an empty spot, which is only about once every ten years. Then the books are opened. It just so happened that the books were opened just when I was being released."

Everyone's first job was in the wet room where the hide was thrown into a solution and left there for a certain length of time. "You can sit and listen to the radio while you're waiting. I dealt with fine furs from all over, even very expensive stuff like mink and Russian sable. It takes so many skins to make a coat. It goes to like $60,000 dollars a coat. It's a wonderful trade. I loved it. But it has a terrible odor. Terrible. Once you get past the odor, you've got it made."

After the wet room, he was moved every three months to a different stage until he had learned the whole process. After that, workers were just sent to wherever they were needed. "At the beginning, I found it very interesting. I loved it. It was the greatest job in the world. Every four days I got a day off. Every six weeks I took home a tenth of my yearly earnings.

"I liked the wet solution best because that's where all the chemistry was and I was very good at chemistry. If you mess it up, you could lose your job even though the process is insured.

"I had no feelings about the animals I worked on. None at all. All I saw on every hide that came in were dollar signs. We worked on a percentage. So many skins, so much money. And everyone had the same attitude. Now, when I see a mink coat coming down the street, I think, 'Boy, somebody sweated like hell to make that.' I know quality. I can appraise skins, I can match skins. I learned a lot on the job. It was the greatest job you could want. And I blew it. That was my second mistake.

"For the first two years, I was a very good worker. I had the best record they'd ever had. I had a nice, expensive apartment on 1st Avenue which I loved. But then I started to neglect my job, taking days off, figuring my father could cover for me, taking advantage. And then, I just got this 'don't give a damn attitude.' I don't know where it came from. I don't know if I was just tired. I know I was very bored with the work. I felt like you could train a monkey to do it. You didn't need a brain. But it was a privilege because it was a closed trade. There were very few Blacks. Maybe five in the whole city were allowed in."

He began to see a lot of a new group of people who worked in Harlem Hospital as technicians. They were all older and earned a lot more money than Gordon and they introduced him to drugs. He began to take days off, half days, whole days, weekends. "I didn't see the habit coming. It comes up slowly. And then, one day, boom, your whole world's shattered. You have no job, you have no friends, your family turns against you. I didn't expect to lose my job. I didn't expect to lose anything. I think I was like having such a good time, drinking and women, you know, that I didn't really care. Nothing mattered. I thought I'd always be able to do something else. I'm not limited. I knew my family would leave me a will. After six months, my money was gone."

The company voted him out. "I felt really bad about that for a long time. I felt I could never have things so easy again. Had I used that time right and used that salary right, I could have accomplished a lot.

"It just broke my father's heart because he was one of the first Blacks to get into that trade. He worked his way up from elevator man until the books finally opened. A nice fellow recommended him and he made it. Everybody liked him. And he was so proud when I got in. They would rotate us and sometimes we were lucky and ended up in the same shop. It was nice because my mother would make lunch and he would bring enough for us both. It was really nice sitting there with him. After work, we'd stop at a bar and have a couple of drinks together. It was really nice. And I lost it. Me and him didn't talk for about two years.

"He never really said mean things to me but I was like bad news. When I came home, he'd leave the room as soon as I came in. Or he'd say, 'You'll never get another job as good. I don't care if you go back and finish college, you'll never get another job as good as that.' That was the whole conversation all the time. That really ticked me off. Because this was the first time I'd ever really given him any disappointment and he took it so hard. It was painful for me, too. I had to change my whole way of living. My mother said, 'Well, Gordon, he'll come through. He's not that bad.' But my father just kept on saying, 'He'll never get another job like that.' He was right."

Gordon seems to have forgotten that he hated the job, that it bored him. Would he have been able to tolerate a lifetime of that work, however much prestige it seemed to have or however well it paid? Or even however much it pleased his father?

"After that, I could never find anything good enough. I'd work for two weeks, then 'Aaw, I don't like this.' I lost my apartment, my fancy apartment. I worked at different jobs for short periods. One was working for a law firm. I did research for them. I got tired of that. I quit and went to work for Parcel Post, on probation. I delivered on the Lower East Side: the Bowery, Delancey Street, Hester Street — a real trash can. They ripped the doors off the truck. Most days, I was lucky to get back in the truck. A real cesspool. I did that for about six months. Then I started taking days off. Finally, I just didn't go back. Never phoned in. Just picked up my final paycheck and walked off. Terrible, right? I got other jobs for short periods. I was getting real disgusted with myself. I couldn't pay my rent. I was losing apartment after apartment. But I wouldn't go back home to live. That was out."

He went to work for a construction company as a carpenter for a job in Alexandria, Virginia. They paid for his hotel and gave him a clothing and food allowance. "It was a real nice area but the drugs were the worst I'd ever seen. This is because dealers hang around sites where there are out-of-town workers who are making big money. They would even get you the stuff on credit. So you find yourself taking things you normally couldn't buy for lack of cash. Now you have the opportunity. And that was my third mistake.

"I never thought of myself as a person hooked on drugs. I'm not. I never went out and did bad things to get drugs. I might have deprived myself but I never deprived anybody else. I'm the one who goes without. It's at a point now where I have to force myself to do things. 'Gordon, go and pay this bill. Gordon, go to the grocery store and buy some food.' There was a period when I didn't have even that much control. I find it really pathetic because I know better. I wasn't raised that way. It hurts me to my heart when I make a stupid mistake like that. Just the mere fact of using a drug is a stupid thing. Because when you come down, you have the same problem. It never goes away. It's just a cop-out, a way to relax. I can take a drink of booze and be as happy, probably even happier, because at least tomorrow, when I wake up, I'll still have money in my pocket. But with this crap...

"I worked the whole contract out but I was ashamed to go home and there was no place else for me to go. That's when I started to travel. I've been traveling for the last seven years and I've worked in almost every city in this country. It's been a crazy life. There's still lots of racism in the South. You had to be careful where you went, where you ate, where you slept. I never slept out. That's something I will never allow to happen to me. Never. I always found a Salvation Army or a shelter of some kind and I could always get some kind of a job.

"I met my friend, Tyler, in Georgia, in a liquor store. He was traveling, too. We hit it off over our first can of beer so we decided to team up. He'd been traveling much longer than me and he'd had lots of experience. It worked fine. If it hadn't been for him, I'd probably still be stuck in a migrant workers' camp, which was really a forced labor camp."

One day, they were hitchhiking in Florida, hoping to get to Georgia when a school bus drove up. "Wanna work?" the driver shouted. "Sure." The bus was full of Haitians and Spanish-speaking people. No one spoke English — except the driver. "He told us we could earn such and such amount of money and we could leave whenever we wanted to. He said we'd ride all night so we wouldn't have to work when we got there. 'Rest up the first day and start to work the next,' he said."

They fell asleep on the bus and wound up in Johnson, South Carolina. As soon as they pulled in, at about 12:00 noon, the driver locked up their backpacks, threw some baskets and a ladder at them and told them to get to work — picking peaches.

"That means, you have to climb a tree with a basket on your chest. By the time you fill it up, it weighs about seventy pounds. You have to come down off the ladder and walk about, maybe, a city block and dump it into a little cart. They told us we'd get 35¢ a basket. Every time you empty a load, they give you a little round disc that says 35¢ on it. They gave us back our packs but we never got any money.

"You could get anything you wanted without money, right there. You just sign your name. They give you dinner, you sign your name. They give you liquor, you sign your name. They give you drugs, you sign your name. The food was great. That's one thing they did, they fed you — so you could work. We stayed in one of the bunkhouses. Only they're not really bunkhouses. They're like slave shacks. Dirty with concrete floors. For beds they had mattresses on concrete slabs and that's it. No pillows, no blankets. The mattresses smelled like a kennel. The restrooms were outside. The showers were outside. Most of the people working there were illegal aliens or running from the law. I never saw any families but I imagine there were some.

"For a radius of about twenty-five miles, there was nothin but peach farms. They say Georgia is the peach state. No, it's not. It's South Carolina. Took me a long time before I ever touched another peach."

At about 1:00 in the morning they climbed over the barbed wire fence. If the police caught them, they would be taken back. "The boss tells the police that you owe them so much money and they rig the books so it looks like you do. And when you get back to that migrant camp, they'll probably beat the Jesus out of you. It was escape, go to jail, or get the Jesus beat out of me. I saw plenty of people there with swollen eyes. I didn't want my eyes to look like that."

They got safely over the fence and walked from there to Columbia, South Carolina, ninety-two miles. They slept in peach groves and on the side of the road. They had no money at all.

"In Columbia, they have these work corners. A guy would drive up in a truck and say he needs ten or twelve people for a job. The work was tedious, a little bit of everything: brick work, moving furniture, moving a pile of dirt from one location to another, moving a pile of sand. The pay, back then, was about $3.00, $3.35 an hour.

"We were living in a Salvation Army shelter. It was nice. We were in for a month. You have to sign up for your bed every night. But if you were there by 11:00 PM, you got in. 11:01, you stayed out. They put you out at about 5:00 AM. because everyone was trying to get to work early. You try to be on the work corner around 5:00 AM so you can be the first one there and get the best job. If you stay in the shelter, they feed you breakfast. Come back for dinner about 5:00 and then go back out.

"We broke up when I went home for a visit. After that, I met Rowetha. She was playing the piano in a church in Beatrice, Alabama. I never go to church but I happened to stop at this one because I was very tired and very hot and I needed to sit down somewhere cool. We started going together and we've been together for almost a year now. I met Tyler again — in a liquor store again, in North Carolina — and the three of us decided to come up here together.

"We've been up here for six months and we can't find any work. That's never happened to me before and it's a very scary thing. Our rent check from the city hasn't come through yet but our landlord is letting us stay because Tyler and me fixed up his basement for him. But we don't know how long that will last.

"Tyler's been acting strange lately. I don't know if it's because of Rowetha or what, but him and me aren't close the way we used to be. I get the feeling he's going to be leaving soon. I'm sorry because he's the only real friend I've had since Calvin, my old high school friend. And I think me and Rowetha will be breaking up soon, too. She wants to go back to Alabama but there's nothing there for me — except the heat. Besides, we're not getting on too well. I told her I'd help her with the fare home because she can't work her way down like I can. But things have been disappearing: my watch, half the money from my last Welfare check, a pocket calculator I got for my sixteenth birthday. That upsets me. That really upsets me.

"I would like to go back to school, complete my studies and get my pharmacist's degree. I'd like to be a pharmacist. I was so good at math. My math teacher encouraged me to be a pharmacist.

"I haven't been home for two years. I'm too embarrassed to go. I never ever want my family to see me do bad. I never go home till I'm feeling really good and I've got my wardrobe together and my appearance together and myself together. Otherwise, I don't go. And the way things are now, I don't know if I'll ever be able to go home again."

MORGAN

"I'm a railroad man.
Railroad is my first love. Like it's in my blood."

He's from Kentucky and speaks with a decided southern accent, a big attractive, outgoing African American, friendly and flirtatious, who laughs and jokes a good deal and says, quite often, about events in his life, "We had a real good time." He has accepted his hardships with remarkable good humor. Sometimes he arrives in torn, dirty jeans which means he has just come from a Temporary Labor job.

I'm a railroad man. Railroad is my first love. Like it's in my blood." He got his first job right after school, through a white boy whose father worked for Penn Central. From the very beginning, he didn't want to be in an office. He wanted to be on the train. He started out as a switchman on a freight train, the only Black in the crew for twelve years. "The other guys treated me pretty good. There was always one who kept calling me 'nigger,' but most of them stood up for me. Pay was the same for both. Promotion, too. We all got on well together. It was like a family. Back then, we had an oil stove on the caboose and we'd bring a skillet, cook dinner and stuff like that. We had a real good time."

His father, a steelworker, died of a heart attack when Morgan was thirteen. "He was real good family. My mother was real good people, too." After his father died, she went to work in a home for the elderly. "I was the oldest son so I had to go to work, too." He says this without rancor or regret.

In the beginning, during his training period, he worked for sixteen hours a day with eight hours off, then back on for another sixteen. The pay was very good but there was no overtime. "You just got paid for a straight eight hours. So the company made a lot of extra money out of us. I averaged about $300 a week, after taxes. I'd say I brought home about $212, gave part to my family and kept about $100. It was a good job in spite of the sixteen hours."

One day he discovered two hobos on the train. They looked peaceful enough, fast asleep, side by side, with a bottle between them. They weren't bothering anybody or taking up any necessary space and he didn't blame them for wanting to ride that train. But he had his orders. "In those days, we didn't think of them as 'homeless.' We thought of them as 'bums.' (Some people still do, I thought.) He radioed ahead to the next stop where the police were waiting and the two men were put off the train like so much baggage. "They were never arrested unless they got violent or made trouble. Which they never did. But you had to be ready. Cause you really didn't know what they would do or how desperate they might be."

He loved being on the road, traveling through the empty countryside, so empty he could see the horizon. "Every now and then, someone would be standing on a porch or working in a field, and they would wave to us like we were old friends. Seems like everybody loves trains." He liked the feeling of freedom the train gave him. "You're on your own. You're runnin the train yourself. I mean, the only orders they give you is to tell you to stop at so and so and pick up some more cars. Like I was a conductor on freight trains and we had to get out of the way for all the passenger trains. That was my job. I felt like it was a real important job."

Usually, he had two days on the road: one day going out and one day coming back. "They'd put you up at a hotel and pay for your room and board. We had a real good time."

He left the railroad to go into the Service. The Vietnam War was still on and he didn't want to wait to be drafted. He wanted to get it out of the way and he wanted to choose what he would do. But he didn't get to choose. He became an assistant in the mess hall with the rank of sergeant. At the last minute he was sent, not to Vietnam, but to Germany. "It was real fine only it was too cold. It was terribly cold. But it was real clean. The Germans are pretty good people. They wrap their garbage up and things like that. Not like they do over here where they just pitch it."

He got back his job on the railroad and put his brothers and sisters through school. Two of his brothers and one of his sisters finished college. "If I could have gone to college, I would be interested, but the kind of job I had on the railroad, I couldn't have made that much more money."

He was married just before he went into the Service. "When I got out, I found my wife was running around with everybody. I tried to get a divorce but she wanted to take just about every penny I earned. So when I heard about a job on the Boston and Maine, I transferred up there. We had a little boy. I haven't seen him for a long time. He's in the Navy now and he went to the Gulf War. I wanted to see him when he came back but I didn't have the fare." He feels bitter about that.

He met Franchette in Boston. "She gave me a real hard time. Me and ladies. I think I'm gonna have a dumb one next time. Seems like all the smart ones are too smart. You're too busy having a lot of mental problems when you could be just enjoying yourself. And her family was in our business all the time."

In the beginning, they went away every weekend: to Cape Cod and New York and Boston. "Dinner and dancing and stuff. We had a real good time. She wanted to adopt a little boy so we did. His name is Patrick. We got him when he was three months old. Today is his second birthday."

At first, they took turns taking care of him. Morgan loved the boy but Franchette became very possessive and Morgan was not allowed to take him out of her sight. One day when Morgan had a day off and she had to go to work, she refused to leave the boy with him. Instead, she took him to the Day Care Center. "The day before we got Patrick, her mother died from an aneurysm in the brain. We had all looked forward to her having a grandson. And then this happened. I think by Franchette losing her mother, she became more attached to this boy."

They never went anywhere anymore. They tried to work it out with a counselor and Morgan waited to see if Franchette would get better. But she kept getting worse. The Boston and Maine dropped a branch line — and Morgan along with it.

He came to New Hope, a good railroad town. But New Hope wasn't a good railroad town anymore. Not where jobs were concerned. He had saved $3,000 but he went through it pretty fast, just paying bills. "This is an expensive place to live. The rent where I was staying was $800 cause I was sure I would find work and I wanted to have a nice place to live. But I couldn't find a job."

Finally he went to work in a slaughterhouse. With pigs. He had a bet with another ex-railway, drinking pal that he wouldn't last three months. The job he had was described as "skinning jowls." The pigs were electrocuted and hung upside down. "When they got to me, they were still quivering. They come along real fast and you couldn't slow them down. A lotta people who worked in the skinning department didn't last very long cause they'd end up with arthritis in their hands from holding those electric knives.

"Where we worked was like an alley way, only inside, but it was always very cold. We were up on a catwalk and there was runnin water so we could keep our knives clean. We wore an apron and boots an there was blood everywhere. We started like about seven in the morning, had a break like about nine, had lunch at twelve and went home at three. I brought my own lunch but I didn't feel much like eating the whole time I was there. That's the worst job I ever had. Paid pretty well. I won my bet but it wasn't for much. In the end, I had to give up my apartment." He swears he'll never eat a sausage or a hot dog or a piece of pork again.

Now he's on unemployment insurance and shares a place with a woman he'd never met before. He saw the ad in the paper of the Emmanuel Baptist church where he often went on Sundays. "Reverend Griggs gave me a good reference because I'm a pretty good guy."

The apartment has five rooms. The two tenants share the kitchen and the bathroom. But his housemate is a problem. "Like she was living there before I was so she acts like it's her apartment. 'But I'm paying half the rent,' I told her. 'An taking up nine-tenths of the livin room,' she said, 'with your beat-up furniture an your beat-up friends. Comin round here whenever they like, stayin up all night and keepin everyone else up, too.' She keeps insulting them, telling them to do their boozing and their whoring somewhere else. 'They got places for that and this ain't one,' she said. The lease is in her name and she keeps threatening to kick me out. If she does, I don't know where I'll go."

He's paying rent with his unemployment insurance but that's good for only thirteen weeks at a time. It ran out once and they gave him a thirteen week's extension. "But if I don't get another extension, I'm going to have to go on Welfare. I'm in a Nurse's Aid training course right now but I don't know if that counts as employment. And I don't know if I'll find a job when it's over. Welfare only pays half the rent. Where will I get the other half?"

He sent his resumé to a man at Amtrak and was told that as soon as a conductor's job was open, he could take the test for it. But last month the man was transferred somewhere else. But where? His replacement is too busy to talk on the phone and doesn't answer Morgan's letters. "I really had hopes because he said he was gonna give me a chance to get back in. Seems like since he moved, I don't know which direction to go in.

"I'm still trying to get work, any kind of work, but the railroad is my first love. I've got a thing for the railroad. It's a skill I have that people on the street don't have so I'd like to utilize it if I can. I had a lotta years on the railroad and I never messed up any company property or had train wrecks or anything like that. It's just unfortunate that I have to be unemployed."

THE UNSKILLED

"Every man's work... is always a portrait of himself."

— *Butler*

Matt (ex-convict)
Spike (victim)
Hughie (petty thief)
James (visionary)
Mark (schoolboy)

The portrait of the unskilled worker is blurred. But for the unemployed among them, it is a blank. For a machine to stand idle is considered deplorable, a terrible waste. For humans to stand idle is regarded as a known fact of economic life which they are expected to endure; or workers are considered somehow to blame though they are no more responsible for their idleness than the machines.

Yet for them, too, as for the skilled, work has its charm. Hughie loved his job with a distributing company. Spike speaks with pride of his work for CETA (Civil Employment Training Administration), cutting grass and shoveling snow. Simone is proud of the clothes she has made, the meals she has cooked, and the tidiness and cleanliness of her apartment.

Like the skilled, they can turn their hands to many different occupations which they learned by doing. Ralph lists carpentry, electricity, heating, air conditioning, house painting, television repair and landscape gardening. Seth has been a nursery school teacher, a hotel waiter, a roofer, an advertising salesman for a newspaper, a drug dealer. Because of their versatility, they could get jobs easily — when there were jobs.

Their lives at the present are grim yet a few take comfort in rosy dreams of the future. Spike, who has suffered from an unhappy home, broken relationships, a damaged leg and a life of perpetual unemployment, insists that he will enjoy a glorious career as a boxer. This will bring him, he believes, the respect which he craves, as well as status and money; and may even enable him to find his real father who left home when Spike was two. James has still grander illusions. He dreams of creating and governing a totally separate and independent black community — with himself as president.

But for most, dreams of the future are pale, timid, as if they cannot, or dare not, hope for much. Simone's idea of a happy life is staying with her boyfriend and working every day. But recently, she turned to God to be born again, as if acknowledging that she needs Him to help her achieve even these modest goals. Seth, a farm boy with a great deal of intelligence and native skills, able to turn from one occupation to another, suddenly took to the road without knowing why; a rejection of his former way of living? a search for a better way? But he knows he will not find it on the road. Matt, an ex-convict, longs to escape from the corrupt life he has been living and to spend his life working with grassroots groups. Hughie, whose life has been brutal, sees his future, like Simone, in minimalist terms:

"To provide for my son and to get back together with my wife."

Yet, for some, the future holds alarming possibilities. Like Ray, Al and Josie, Matt predicts a time of violence and chaos if the threatened cuts go through.

Only Mark, a very thoughtful and perceptive African American teenager, cherishes a dream which is both extremely ambitious but perhaps not wholly unrealistic. A devout Muslim, he believes that God put him on earth to do something positive for somebody. Deprived of an education, indeed of a normal life, by the violence and depravity of his schoolmates and neighborhood peers, he longs to become a judge in order to help reform them.

Society has robbed these victims of their portraits. But their desperate longing for a better future — beyond the soup kitchen and the Welfare check — gives us a glimpse of how their portraits might look.

MATT

"I'd like to get a full-time job and spend the rest of my time doing grassroots work. But I'd like to feel secure first, know that I'm not going to be pushed out on the street again."

His interview was the longest, stretching over many days, and the most detailed, as if he had total recall. He had a part-time job as a parking lot attendant and we met in his little booth where he had a heater, a tiny television set and a coffee pot. Sometimes I brought coffee cake or doughnuts or cigarettes; and sometimes friends of his stopped by to say hello or to bum a cigarette or borrow money. He is clearly well liked and is active in PEOPLE FIRST.

I've spent a lot of time in jail. In fact, you could say I was raised in jail. Only they called it Collins Court, that housing Project on the other side of the highway. It's separated from the respectable part of town just like a prison. And everybody in there was a potential convict."

The Project was mixed — Italian and Black. Matt is Irish but, against the Blacks, all Whites closed ranks in constant race warfare. "There were the white Lords and the black Eagles. I was 'invited' to join the Lords at the age of twelve. I had no choice. I got a first-rate education in smashing windows, ripping tires and beating up people with stones and bats and knives. I also became an expert in breaking and entering. I was small for my age and quick. I could get in and out of tight places real fast.

"There are plenty of middle-class people who would do illegal things if they thought they could get away with it. You can see it in little ways right around you. There's a place in North Hope where the rich people live that looks like the city dump: old refrigerators, stoves, beds, mattresses. People from the ghetto aren't going way out there to dump that stuff. It's your fancy 'middle class.' And those signs in the big stores advertising 'Senior Citizen Discounts' — that means they're going to jack the prices up 25% and then take 10% off. That's middle-class robbery. Take the supermarkets. Today's the first of the month so prices are going up because that's when the Welfare checks arrive. And they're going up again on the third when the food stamps come. That's middle-class robbery, too. Fact is, there isn't any middle class. There's just rich and poor. And the rich are getting richer and the poor are getting poorer."

His father left home when Matt was four. Matt never saw him again because his mother never let his father into the house again. When Matt quit school his junior year, she wouldn't let him into the house either.

He lived with a friend. "We had a hard time looking for jobs. It was easier to look for girls. We'd find a bottle and go out on Friday nights with guys I'd known for years who had quit school, too. It was summer. We didn't need much money. The beach was free, the car cost $50.00, we all pitched in for the booze and, for entertainment, we had the girls."

For a while, he worked as a superintendent in an apartment house where he lived rent free but received no pay. What he did receive were phone calls at all hours of the day and night from the other tenants. They were Welfare recipients demanding that he repair the elevator, clean up the vomit on the stairs, fix the outside light, stop the drunks from singing in the halls, stop the fight in 12B, and stop that maniac from jumping off the roof. Matt worked round the clock without pay. But soon he lost even that. When the Welfare payments were cut for the first time, all the tenants were evicted. And so was Matt. He had no job and no home. It was frightening. He began to take drugs pretty regularly.

He lived with a friend again and together they started on a life of crime. They began by getting school boys to steal pots and pans from Macy's for them. When two of the boys were arrested, Matt and his friend moved over to Cutlery. Knives went into their pockets and up their sleeves and up their trouser legs. When the knives were no longer on display, they turned to more expensive items: radios, tape recorders, stereos. They were caught several times.

"I learned a lot about jails. County jails starve you to death. In one prison, they had a Substance Abuse Treatment Unit. That meant that everyone on drugs got locked up — except for three hours a day — six days a week. On the seventh day, they locked you up for twenty-four hours and brought your meals to the cell. You were never allowed out of it without handcuffs on. That was the 'treatment.'"

In another jail, he was sent to "segregation" for hitting a guard, which was the very worst crime imaginable, regardless of the provocation. And segregation, in this instance, was the worst punishment that could be inflicted without drawing blood.

He was completely stripped and thrown into a cell with no mattress, no water and no toilet. Instead there was a hole in the floor that flushed automatically and not very often. For breakfast he was given two slices of dry bread, a cup of oatmeal with no sugar, no milk and a cup of water. At lunch he had a lettuce leaf with, sometimes, a cut-up carrot on top, two slices of dry bread and a cup of water. For supper he had breakfast again. He was so cold he couldn't sleep and was chronically starved and dehydrated. His friends told him later that he was there for twenty-eight days. When he came out, he was taken to the Infirmary. He had lost twenty-five pounds and couldn't walk.

After prison, he was still shooting cocaine. He wasn't working, wasn't trying to work and he was stealing again. The police knew it. "I couldn't walk down the street without being stopped. I was arrested like four times in one month for possession of narcotics. I was selling syringes. I could make around $75 in five minutes. It's the insanity of wanting the stuff so bad you don't care what you do to get it. We lied to people for money. We beat people up for money. We flimflammed people. We sold boxes filled with rocks and claimed it was a VCR. We did it anywhere in the city, any place where people have money and think they're getting a good deal. You can tell just by looking at them. But it wasn't bringing in much.

"And then I discovered the University. Oh boyeeeee. Lovely, new computers. All over the place. Especially in that big, old building on Emerson Street."

I bolted upright. "Emerson Street? 21 Emerson Street?"

"Across from the gym? Yeah. That's right."

"You stole my husband's computer!" I shouted.

"I did? Was it a Mac Plus?"

"It was."

"Was that your husband's? I'm sorry."

"That was fifteen years of hard work you stole."

"I'm sorry."

"And his wasn't the only one. You went back the next night and cleaned out the whole building!"

"I did. Then I went back for the third time and got busted. But tell your husband I'm sorry."

Luckily, he had not taken the diskettes.

The next night he turned up at the soup kitchen with some mysterious device to hitch to a computer. "For your husband," he said. I refrained from asking where and how he got it.

Finally, he was hired by a drug dealer and was able to rent an apartment and buy a car. Through the drug dealers, he got a job with a big international syndicate to move guns from New Hope to New York for resale. Now hc was making really big money. But he got caught and sentenced to three years. "They were lenient because I wasn't a big fish and they thought maybe they could get me to roll over on someone they really wanted. After I got out, they followed me everywhere. I had friends that I couldn't even hang out with anymore. They told me, 'Don't come around because every time you do, so does the FBI.'"

He was sent to the federal penitentiary in Terre Haute, Indiana. "That was the toughest place I've ever been in. All the cliques are there. They have The Aryan Brotherhood which are the white guys, The Latin Kings which are the Spanish guys and The Muslims which are the black guys. If you don't belong to one of them or to a nationally-known motorcycle club or you're not affiliated with one of them, you're a victim. All these organizations started in prison except for the Muslims. They began in Harlem in the forties, then seeped into the prisons. They're militant and violent — like everyone else. Especially in prison. They protect their own."

As soon as Matt got there, he attached himself to people he knew through his drug and gun-dealing connections. He was affiliated with

Hell's Angels but he wasn't a member. "My friends covered me so that other people wouldn't vamp on me.

"How you're treated by the other prisoners depends on who you are and what you're in for. It's easy to know because there are inmates who work in the office. I've seen killings in jail and I think prisoners kill each other for sex crimes, debts, informing and kidnapping kids. Rape, not murder, is the bottom of the pit because everyone has a wife or a girlfriend or a sister or a daughter. Prisoners are angry anyway, mainly because they're locked up. If you're out in the free world, you might sit down with a beer to watch the news on TV. You might see some child rapist and say, 'They should burn that sucker.' But you're not going to go out and shoot him. But you put that same person in jail and put that rapist in there with him and that rapist is dead. The guy'll kill him." Murderers get the best treatment — from the inmates *and* from the guards.

Prisoners kill with knives which they make out of anything they can get. "Someone on maintenance steals a piece of plexiglass and smuggles it to someone in the property shop. He sharpens it on the concrete, smuggles it into the side shop and cuts it up into strips when the supervisor isn't looking. Then he smuggles it right back out. Everything gets passed from one guy to another. It never stays in anyone's hands long enough for anyone to get caught with it. A metal detector won't pick up plexiglass.

"I saw two murders in prison. Both were for money. It was someone I knew each time and each time, I knew who did it. One guy, Crocker, was killed because he had paid someone to testify in a trial for him. He paid the first $2500 but when he was found guilty, he refused to pay the rest. Both men were in prison together. There was a contract out on Crocker and he was stabbed to death. The murderers in prison always get caught. But there's no value to a prisoner's life. Outside, you could get the death sentence for committing murder. Inside, the average sentence for murder is four years."

One very young prisoner who was found bleeding on the floor of the bathroom, claimed that someone had stabbed him. In the infirmary, he told the truth. "Those Hell's Angels are wringing me out for money because I owe them $200. They're charging me $5 a day just to stay alive. I'm scared for my life. They've got drugs all over the place and they're all killers anyway. I'm afraid they're gonna kill me in here." He had stabbed himself with a soda can but it was only a superficial wound. He named names. They transferred him to another prison.

Matt was paid protection every week to make sure nobody hurt an inmate who was in for molesting little boys. He could promise this because he had friends who were Latin Kings and they more or less controlled that dorm.

He came close to being attacked himself once. "Someone tried to put a contract out on me because, years before, I was messing with his girlfriend. When he got locked up with me, he went to these black guys and said, 'Two cartons of cigarettes if you do something to this guy.' The black guys were friends of mine. They came to me, even gave me one of the cartons. 'You gotta do something to this guy,' they said, 'cause he's gonna try to pay somebody else.'

"I tried. I put two master padlocks in a sock. They sell padlocks in the commissary because you have to lock your stuff up or it's gone. The guards don't care. 'You were robbed? Tough luck.' They caught me with the padlocks, gave me fifteen days in the hole and took away fifteen days good time. I'd been counting the months on my fingers until I could get out."

This time the hole wasn't bad. "You get recreation for an hour a day, you get showers and you get books. They have a bookcart that comes around. I read Stephen King. He's a very popular prison author. Any time

Stephen King comes out with a book, everybody in prison wants it. He's got more imagination and originality than most. I used to read Grisham and David Cootes and Bradbury. And those stupid books that came out in the '70s, promoting Satanism, saying that all those movie stars and singers were devil worshippers and how we should live for pleasure and not be subservient to any higher being. I didn't mind being in the hole. I needed a rest.

"I didn't worry too much about a contract on me because a) you never go anywhere alone and b) I hung around with guys that were monsters. I don't know if their mothers were on steroids when they were pregnant or what, but these guys were huge. And they were my friends. They had this gigantic room full of weights and all we did in free time was lift weights. We never had any problems in the gym. We had our part of the weight room, the black guys had their part of the weight room and the Spanish guys had their part of the weight room. If you didn't fit in anywhere, you just didn't go there."

Matt kept using drugs in prison. The guards knew it was going on but they ignored it because it helped to control the inmates. "If everyone's sitting around stoned, they're not going to be stabbing each other. But we couldn't get any rolling papers in prison because they didn't want us rolling our own marijuana. So I learned how to make a little marijuana pipe out of a pencil and a playing card. You can only do one hit at a time but your marijuana lasts longer that way. I also learned how to make wine out of sugar, orange juice and yeast. I learned a lot in prison.

"Prison guards are too scared to steal and too stupid to get a real job. I see them as criminals if they think they can get away with it. With the Republican administrations we've been having, they get away with more than they used to. There's more brutality. That's probably why there's so much trouble in prisons now. Because all the guards want is more pay and less hours and more guards. We wouldn't need more guards if they treated prisoners like human beings. And they don't deserve any more money. In fact, they don't deserve what they're getting now.

"Prisons are terribly overcrowded and there's a lot better ways to handle crime. There are different kinds of offenses. There are the sex offenders, the killers, the torturers. You know you can't rehabilitate them so don't even try. Just lock them up and throw away the key. Then there are people who steal because of financial need. And there are people who steal because they have a drug habit or an alcohol habit. Those people can be helped. If they need treatment, give them treatment."

After prison, Matt got a job at The Eagle Café. He worked at the bar at night and during the day he was out stealing: aluminum ladders, fiberglass ladders, building materials, office equipment. The owner bought it all. Matt was making lots of money and spending very little. Drinks were free at the bar and he was trying to stay away from drugs. "I'd stay away from them for maybe two or three weeks and then I'd go on a little coke run for a week, then get straight again for two or three weeks, then go on another coke run. I thought I could handle it but I really couldn't and I didn't want to admit it."

The boss owed him a lot of money but refused to pay because the bar was losing money. "I told him he *had* to pay me because I was quitting. 'You can't quit,' the boss said, 'because you're fired.' He paid me some back salary but he still owed me around $18,000."

Matt had his own set of keys for the bar. "One Sunday, at around 3:00 AM, I went back and cleaned out the place. I took $19,000, a couple of bottles of good vodka, a bottle of Jack Beam and all the change the boss used to throw into the spittoon behind the bar. There must have been like $100 worth of quarters in there. I filled my pockets."

It was drizzling outside. There was a man Matt had known since they were boys and he knew he was sleeping out in a mini park with a friend. "I found them, cold and wet, gave them the booze and emptied my pockets. 'Have a nice Monday, you guys.'"

Some of the money Matt stole didn't belong to the boss. It belonged to other people. "They put a raid on me. They're not the kind who call in the cops. They take care of things themselves."

One Sunday morning, Matt was in Burger King when he suddenly realized that "they" were all around him — inside, sitting at tables, outside, sitting in cars, waiting for him to leave. Just then, a policeman came in and Matt struck up a conversation. He knew the policeman would leave by the underground garage and come out on the next street without ever going outside. "I'll take a walk with you," Matt said.

"My biggest problem has been gaps in my work history unless I lie or leave out the dates on my resumé. But I often get caught on that. It's getting harder and harder because the job market's much tighter now and they're much fussier. I know a guy with a college degree who's working as a security guard."

Matt lives on his part-time job at the parking lot and the soup kitchen and works with PEOPLE FIRST to stop the Welfare cuts. "It will be a nightmare if the cuts go through. And they will. They'll cut the poor so they won't have to tax the 'middle class,' so they won't have to give up that second house on the Cape or that second car or that trip to France next summer. They'll need to get away because it's going to be really nasty for them out there, picking their way through the human garbage on the streets. PEOPLE FIRST is trying to get that message across. But I don't think they're listening.

"I've been lucky because I just got this part-time job through an ex-inmate pal of mine. The owner gave me this heater and the little TV set so it's quite comfortable. I know practically everybody that walks these streets: the homeless, the alcoholics, the drug addicts. I even see the gang that was after me for the bar robbery. They come to the bar next door and park their cars with me. Some of them shake my hand, 'You look good. You got yourself together.'

"I have a lot of friends on the police force now because of this job. Yesterday, when it was raining all day, the cop outside said, 'Mind if I come in for a minute?' I said, 'Come on in. The heater's on. Relax. Watch TV. Have a cigarette. I'll make some coffee.' He told me all about his marital troubles and his kid that's hooked on heroin.

"My drinking's been better but it would be even better if I didn't drink at all. I used to go to AA meetings but I still drink. And I'll never be safe from my drug addiction. Narcotics Anonymous has been my only treatment but I'm lapsing now because of my job and my work with PEOPLE FIRST. It's okay because I have NA people that come by here and check on me and there are drug people I can call on. I'd go every night if I could.

"I'd like to get a full-time job and spend the rest of my time doing grass-roots work. But I'd like to feel secure first. Know that I'm not going to be pushed out on the street again."

SPIKE

"I felt like nobody's got a place for me.
I gotta be out there on the street on my own."

He is a solidly-built African American, open and demonstrative, with a huge smile and a hearty laugh. But he is also short-tempered which leads him to acts of violence. He wants desperately to think well of himself and to be well thought of by others. But this is difficult given his disreputable record. He believes, with good reason, that life has been hard on him which leads to feelings of frustration, paranoia and anger.

There's no one I feel close to. My father left home when I was two. I saw him once or twice when I was older. The last time was when I was nine. He brought me presents. I wanted to see him more but my mother and stepfather wouldn't allow it." After his father left, Spike and his mother lived with his grandmother in Montjoy. She loved him and took good care of him and he loved her. But his mother married again when Spike was around four, and they moved back to New Hope. After that, he was left alone most of the time.

"When my two brothers came along, it was like a hardship to me. At seven or eight, I was taking care of them while my stepfather and my mother would be out workin. She worked all the time I was growin up. She was a waitress. Every Thursday or Friday, she would take me and my two step-brothers shoppin and buy us model cars and toys to keep us busy while she was at work. After a while, there were more brothers. I took care of all of them.

"My mother and her husband fought all the time. He beat her and he beat me. He wasn't drunk. He was just a jealous man. He was jealous of me, mostly, because I wasn't his son. And plus when she wanted to buy me somethin, he'd get upset. He didn't beat his own children much at all. He beat me all the time.

"We lived on Beacon Avenue. It wasn't a neighborhood. It was a car avenue. Nuthin but car companies and gas stations all the way out. Maybe that's why I ended up likin cars so much. School was mixed. The neighborhood was mixed. There was no racial problem. We all went to school together, played together. I liked to go over to my friends' house. The air was nicer over there."

One morning, when Spike was about eight, he felt a cold draft in his face. He got up and went into his parent's room. There was a blast of air coming from the window, the curtains were flying, there was glass on the floor and his mother was lying in bed with her head against the headboard. She looked at him and said, "Your father took my head and bashed it into the window."

Spike had to take the window to Slansky's glass shop to be fixed. "You fix that window, Spike," Mr. Slansky said. He showed Spike how and told him to keep the money. Spike bought some candy for his brothers but when he got home, his mother accused him of taking the money from her pocketbook. That night, his stepfather gave him a terrible whipping.

Another time his father had his mother down on the couch, choking her. "She told me to get a knife because she wanted to get the man offa her. But I was scared he'd take the knife from me and stab us both. I had to just stand there and watch. They still be together. He's like twenty-two years older than my mother. I don't know why she stays with him."

When Spike came home from school, he shut himself up in his room because he was afraid of his stepfather. Often he stayed after school to help the teacher, just to keep from going home. He loved school but his work was falling off "because of all the aggravation and torment my stepfather was givin me.

"Saturday come, I had to clean the whole house, wash all the pots and pans and dishes that was stacked up to the ceiling. My brothers was still in the bed, sleepin. There'd be butcher's knives on the wall and I'd be lookin at them, lookin from the big knives to the little knives. And I would say to myself, 'Which one will I use to stab him with?'"

He got little jobs after school, shining shoes and washing dishes at Warner's Drug Store but his brothers kept taking the money out of his room. He asked his mother to keep it for him and she said, "I'll give it to your father. Let him lock it up." But when Spike wanted his money for a pair of shoes, his stepfather said, "Don't you know, you have to pay bills, lectric bills an gas bills an stuff?" "At eleven years old, I had to help pay bills. So therefore I couldn't get the things I wanted, the shoes I needed for school, the sneakers I needed for gym. He took my money. Even the money I got from my job at the Montgomery Community House: $50 for cleanin up, helpin with the kids an stuff like that. All that money went into the box. His children were treatin me bad, too, takin my things. I was bein treated so doggish, I couldn't wait for the time when I got ready to leave home."

He began to run away. He didn't know where he was going. He just ran. His stepfather came after him with a belt. He even sent the cops after him. Spike ran along the rooftops and stayed up there, almost went to sleep up there. Once the cops found him walking the streets and dragged him home. His stepfather locked him in his room until he was ready to beat him. Spike ran away every chance he got.

He ended up in the Juvenile Detention Center for running away and for being "mischievous." "They locked you up at night and if you were mischievous, they tied you to a pole and made you stay there for a half hour to a whole hour. Sometimes the cuffs would be so tight that your hands would swell up. I didn't try to break out like most of the other guys. Because where would I go?" The judge asked him whether he wanted to go home or to the Boys' School. "I looked at Ma. I looked at the judge. 'I think I'll go to the Boys' School,' I said."

He stayed at the Boys' School for about six months. He enjoyed it. The boys were given brand new khaki pants and khaki shirts, just like an army uniform, and boots for work and shoes for church on Sundays. They even gave the boys a small allowance. They went to school in the morning and had jobs in the afternoon. Spike worked in the hospital belonging to the school, got the mail, made sure it was delivered, worked as a maintenance man, mopped the floors and kept the place up to par. He felt good about that. But he got into fights with the boys and even with one of the staff. "He hit me. Right in the mouth. He did that a lot. They're not sposed to hit us." They moved Spike to another cottage for a while. When he came back, the boys were glad to see him. "They liked me!" he said.

"One day Mr. Perry, the cottage father, told me: 'If you wanted, you could be a good fighter.' God bless his soul. He was a white guy, very kind, very strong. Every time he seen me, he always gave me a hug. Like I was his own son. Like he wanted to try to help me out. Like he's saying, I'm a pretty good fellow. He told me if I wanted to be a professional boxer, he would sponsor me."

Once, Spike was put in "the cubes" — the cubicles under the hospital — because he was fighting with everyone. "That was like being in prison. Like staying locked up in a four by four by yourself. You come out to eat, have a shower, have a cigarette. Then you go back in. I was fourteen.

"One night, I snuck off the grounds and went over the fence to my grandmother's house. She told me, 'Son, do me this one favor. Go back.' She said it so I did it. Everything she ever told me was correct. I don't think I seen my mother all the time I was there.

"When I got home, seein how my stepfather was, I started getting really rambunctious. I wasn't goin to school. I was goin wild, doin crazy things. I was with a gang. We were stealin, we were drinkin, we stole cars, we broke in, we robbed. I got into fights with boys on the streets, with friends, with strangers, with other gangs. But what that was really about was that I was angry about my stepfather. All this anger really started comin out. I just wanted to stop anybody from jumpin on me. I had enough from my stepfather. Wasn't nobody else goin to do it to me.

"Later, when I was in high school, my parents were really givin me hell. Like they didn't want me to go to school, didn't want me to learn nuthin. Didn't want me to work neither. Didn't want me to do nuthin but be a failure. My stepfather was like, 'You done had your way here long enough. It's about time for you to participate with the family.'

"I was busy tryin to do other things, tryin to stay out of trouble, tryin to be constructive, doin little jobs: shinin shoes, emptyin trash for the old folks down the street. Sometime they would give me things. I cumulated so much stuff, my stepfather said, 'Where you get this from?' He was givin it out to my brothers. I watched him put his knee through my dart board and throw it in the trash can, saying it was dangerous for my brothers. But they was never around. This was what my father gave me and I was tryin to enjoy it — by myself. Even the red wagon that I put together real good, that I've never even used. It was more like a show model because my father gave it to me. My stepfather gave it to my brothers. They smashed it up and he put it in the trash. So everything I ever owned was like being destroyed on me: my clothes, my belongings, everything."

He still tried to help his mother and often took care of the younger boys. One day, he was helping her peel potatoes. One of his brothers was bothering a younger brother and making him cry. Spike kept telling him to stop but he kept on until Spike swung at him, forgetting that he had a knife in his hand. The boy laughed and laughed and said, "Ha ha, you missed." Spike went for him again and this time the knife cut the boy's shirt. "They took me to New Hope Hospital to see the psychiatrist. It was the time Martin Luther King was killed and the cops kept askin me all kinda dumb questions like was I upset about Martin Luther King. I was gettin sicka answerin those stupid questions. I said, 'I'm tired. I'm goin home.' I ran down the hall and they tackled me, policemen, detectives, everyone. They gave me somethin to calm me down and took me to Spring Valley Mental Hospital. My mother tried to tell them that I was emotionally disturbed and that I can't accept rejection.

"She was always saying stuff like that. One day, I snapped at her. 'You go roun tellin people that I got a motional problem, that I'm disturbed an a misfit. You know why? Because of you and your husbin. I mean, this man been beatin on me, hittin on me, and me watchin you gettin yourself killed by him. That's enough to drive anybody up the wall. You should have got rid of that man a long time ago.' She tried to say that he's a this an he's a that. I said, 'He's a nuthin. Nuthin but a old man that goes to work in a gun factory and brings home a little bit of nuthin of money. Very seldom we eat chicken in this house or eat meat in this house. Every day in the week we're eatin black-eyed beans and ketchup, tryin to spice em up. Only real meal we ever have is on Sundays, like chicken and mash potatoes. Rest of the time we eatin nuthin but beans.'"

He often tried to get in touch with his real father who was a deputy sheriff in Massachusetts but he couldn't get any information from his family, "because my aunts and them had a little bad record. And then, too, they felt like if he found out what my stepfather had done to me, my real father would end up comin to kill him. That's why I wanted to become a boxer. I figured by being a boxer, I could work my way to Massachusetts. My mother said there were other things to do beside boxin an that was all I ever thought about. I guess that was her way of tryin to knock me from bein successful.

"Beside that, I wanted to be a good mechanic. I loved cars. That's what I studied a lot. That probably came from livin on Montgomery Avenue with all those car companies, an my mother buying me model cars when I was little."

He had his first taste of jail at sixteen for fighting in a bar. He wasn't drunk. The bartender got foul-mouthed and he got foul-mouthed back. "That's when all the chaos started. My cousins were fightin, too. We were all arrested but everybody got bailed out but me. I went to the Montgomery Avenue jail. Nobody knew I was there. Nobody tried to get me out. Nuthin. I stayed in there for thirty days. Being in that jail was just like being locked up in a small closet, waiting for breakfast, lunch, dinner. An recreation — sometimes. But that was just sittin in the Day Room watchin TV. No sports, nuthin like that." When he got home, his mother looked at him and said, "Where you been?"

"My parents started talking crazy to me again an I left. I felt like nobody's got a place for me. I got to be out there on the street on my own."

He met Germaine at a party one night. "She gave me a kiss and told me to come by." She was nineteen. Spike was sixteen. They had their first child when he was about seventeen.

"I tried to do everything I could to make sure the baby had food and milk. I got warehouse jobs: moving food, loading it, distributing it, moving furniture and everything else. Even drove a van. Wasn't paid much but I made good money cause I worked so many hours. At my age, it wasn't so bad. I was always a hustler."

He worked in the CETA program for two years when he was nineteen, cutting the grass on the Green and in the parks. "I enjoyed that. The boss was crazy about me. He loved the way I worked, how fast I cut the grass, all nice and neat, all around the Green and the crosswalks; how fast I got the snow plowed out, how fast I shoveled. I went to school at night for a training course in mechanics. We were paid for going.

"Only trouble was Germaine. She kept tryin to impress her friends that she's so high society, showin off to them all the time. I'm tryin to pay the rent, make ends meet, buyin Pampers by the case to make sure my kid had enough. And she's givin them to her girlfriends and spendin lots of money on clothes and stuff like that. Even when she had my second daughter, she still acted like a big child. So I left. It was hard for me to do it because of my girls.

"Sometimes I'd go by at night just to see the kids tucked away in bed.

I just never was upset long as my kids were okay. My parents looked down at my kids, especially my stepfather, like they were nuthin. The older one graduated from high school. The other one's in college. I'm a grandfather." He shows me their pictures with pride.

He worked on and off at Temporary Labor doing mechanical work, carpentry and painting, and started to train as a fighter. "I liked it. I was good at it. It was just about the only thin that kept me goin."

He was living all around town, with different women. "There was a cop's sister, Louella. I stayed with her the longest. Almost eleven years. She had a job in the Financial Building in the evening, cleanin floors and bathrooms an stuff an in the day time, she was a private duty nurse. She's eight years older than me. In the beginnin she was a nice person, a warm-hearted woman. Everythin was so sweet till she got money crazy.

"I had a wall collapse on me on a construction site eight years ago today. And I'm still tryin to get my life straightened out. I was hurt very bad. In fact, I'm lucky to be still here and still walkin. Not 100%, and sometimes my leg still bothers me. This disables me from work. It's eight years I been outta work.

"At the time the accident happened, I was workin two jobs: at construction durin the day, an washin dishes an cleanin the kitchen an everythin else at Karl's Kitchen at night. In between, I worked out in the gym. I was feelin just fine, workin out, gettin ready for the fight on March 5th. I hoped to go on fightin because my kids were comin out of school and I wanted them to be happy and have somethin. And then, because of the accident, I couldn't do it. Tears came down my face when the time came because I couldn't fight. Because I failed the people I'd promised.

"That was when things fell apart between Louella and me. My lawyer was gonna ask for a million dollars for me. And then, suddenly, he turned around and wouldn't take the case. So therefore, right then and there, I knew. Somebody was gettin paid off to do me in.

"One night Louella wanted me to go outside to get some exercise. I went but I knew something was fishy, the way she was like pushin me out the door. And when I got out there, this is when I seen the whole show. This car followed me for like ten minutes. Never came up, never passed, nuthin. Just stayed behind. That was my boss and the insurance company and everybody else in that car, makin sure that I could walk so they wouldn't have to pay out all this Compensation. An that was my fiancée, pushin me out the door. The case was, like, demolished. But I'm still tryin to get my Compensation.

"I had a nervous breakdown and nearly committed suicide. I overdosed on medication because Louella had made me so upset. I was just so full of pressure. I was gonna take my crutches and hit her just as hard as I could. I didn't. I had to take my pills. That's when I overdosed.

"I had Disability money comin in so I moved out — to the Project. It was terrible. People drinkin, people on drugs, people fightin all the time. Louella wantin to make up. She kept comin roun pesterin me. And then one night, she stole my wallet with all my social security money. I was mad, real mad. So I told the police and they locked her up.

"After she got out, that's when I noticed a change in the place. The tenants started harassing me, threatenin me, fightin with me. Because she had told everyone that I snitched on her. I wasn't thrown out of the Project like some people say. I took myself out.

"Now every time I move around, somebody's followin me: drug dealers, people from the Project, even people I don't know. I think they want to kill me. There's a car that follows me at night, a black car with a white top. I'm scared but I can't go to the police. How I'm gonna prove anythin? I don't know who they are. I don't even know the license number.

"I stayed in the train station. I was afraid to go to the shelter. Too many people that knew me would be there and start harrassin me. I would end up gettin into trouble and I was tryin to stay out of trouble. I've been doin this all my life. Runnin. But see, I'm gettin tireda runnin.

"I'm havin trouble findin a place to live because I have to be so choicy. I don't want to be around drunks and junkies and people wantin to fight me. I'll just start fightin again. Like at my cousin's. She let me stay there last night and she made me so mad, I beat her up. Cause she's spendin all her money on drugs an her two little girls are sleepin on the floor with the rats. They were so glad to see me. I brought them a pizza an everythin. I want to help them so bad. But what can I do? If I had my Compensation, I could buy things for them: decent clothes, even beds so they wouldn't have to sleep on the floor. They wanted me to stay with them. But if I go back there, I hate my cousin so much, I'm afraid I'll kill her.

"I'm gonna start lookin for work again. And when I get back on my feet, I'm goin back to the gym again. An this time I'm not slippin back in the corner. This time, I'm gonna stay right there in the middle and deal with it.

"If I had a choice of a job, what I would like to do is maybe be a counselor for people that have problems like I had. But I gotta get my GED first. (General Equivalency Diploma: high school equivalent. Classes are free.)

"I wasn't brought up in religion. I was just brought up goin to church. I like goin to church. I pray for the day I can go to school, that I'll have the strength and get my GED. But right now, I'm out on the street again, wanderin around like I'm waitin to be shot."

HUGHIE

"All I really want is just a basic job and a nice place to stay and provide for my son."

He is a handsome African American and is evidently Simone's boyfriend for he sometimes comes to the Rec Center and the soup kitchen with her. They usually keep to themselves, away from the others. In the soup kitchen, he appeared rather hostile but during the interview, he seemed to relax and was surprisingly forthcoming. He is twenty-eight and has, perhaps, one of the most depressing life stories.

My father was incarcerated for killing a man when I was between nine and ten. I didn't know about it until he'd been in prison for about a year or two. I never really knew what happened and I don't remember how I felt about it. Me and my father never really had no father-son relationship anyway. We never really had no talks, nothing because he was never there. He was off selling drugs. He was a big-time drug dealer back in the 70's. We was rich. My father always had houses and restaurants and stuff like that. He took care of us financially. We lived on Charleston Avenue back when it was fast with money and drugs. Like New York.

"My mother was an alcoholic. She never had to work. My father used to beat her. He beat all of us. They never really had no marriage. He'd just come home, beat her, beat us. It was bad. So they divorced. Matter of fact, he had other women while they was married and she knew about it. But she was scared of him. She turned alcoholic because of that. But in the last two years, she stopped. By herself. And now she's into church and she's doing real good. I see her maybe once or twice a week. She couldn't hardly walk because of the alcohol. Now she can walk and she's going to church and everything. She doesn't work. She's on Social Security."

The family lost everything when his father went to jail. They came from Brooklyn and had no relatives in New Hope. "There was eight of us left with my mother. She never had a job because he was taking care of us. And suddenly we had nothing. That encouraged me to indulge in criminal activities.

"When my father was home, it was school every day, church every week. But when he left, I just let loose. My mother couldn't control me because she was drinking at the time. So everything went wild.

"I was tossed around in school because we moved a lot. I never graduated but I have a GED from prison.

"Ever since I was young, I been back and forth to prison. Up until six months ago. I was in for stealing and drugs and petty larceny. They sent me to Long Lane for juveniles, they sent me to group homes, all of that. It was bad. I had friends who were in trouble with me, guys in the neighborhood who were about my age but started before I did.

"The longest prison term I had was three years. I was in for selling drugs and attempted burglary. I was already on parole when this happened. I already did five hits before this. Mostly for five or six months.

"My worst experience in prison was the riot between the Blacks and the Hispanics. It started over each of them trying to rule the prison. We were out in the courtyard and they surrounded us and started pulling out knives and stuff. There was like 1500 prisoners in that jail and they was all in it. Couple of people got stabbed. Lotta people got hurt. I got caught up in it but I wasn't hurt. I didn't get the sack. That's what they call the punishment. If you get caught up in a riot and they have a lotta cameras there, and they can identify you, they ship you out of state to one of the worst prisons in the country with another ten years added on to your sentence. And you're separated from the brothers and can't reach your family.

"It could start over a petty argument, say between me and a Hispanic. And the Hispanics want to get me. They jump me and some of the brothers help me. It could start over TV shows, anything. Whites weren't involved in this one.

"I wasn't worried about violence in prison. I been there so many times, I know so many people. I wasn't worried about the guards neither. They just sorta dog you out. A lot of them are racists. I'm not speaking for all of them. Some of them are like that. They get on you for any little thing. Get you disciplinary points which make you stay in longer and all for no reason. Antagonize you so you'll go off and then they put you in the hole. Stuff like that. You have to adjust.

"They've got college courses, school computers, all that. I had two years of high school. You can sign up. It was good. It was quite professional. I liked it. I like math and reading. Reading is my favorite subject.

"I've been out for six, seven months. I got out, like most people, with a positive attitude. Start looking for a job. You don't find none. Then back into the same old pattern.

"I worked for Universal Distributors before I was incarcerated. It's like the Stop and Shop warehouse. It's a good job. I loved that job. You select stuff from the warehouse, take it to shipping and they send it to Stop and Shop. I don't know if they'd hire me back. Once you've been incarcerated, they consider you a little risky. I don't put that on applications. Some people check on you. I put it on for the good jobs, government jobs, stuff like that, you know. But basic jobs, no. But so far, I haven't had any luck.

"My father's out now. He lives in New Hope. He goes to see my mother and asks her for money. He comes to the kitchen sometimes. I see him maybe twice a week. We say 'Hi.' That's all.

"I'm trying to be positive. Two or three months ago, I stopped getting high and stuff like that. I'm doing temporary jobs and looking for a steady job. I'm still going to agencies, filling out applications. I'd like a trade. But my problem was like having no place to stay. I don't mind not getting a job so much but having no place to rest, or take care of your hygiene, it's hard. So I was trying to establish that first. I started living with Simone in her apartment after she broke up with her boyfriend. We're both getting City Assistance and I do whatever jobs the agency gives me. But it's just daily work. It doesn't get you anywhere.

"I don't have any idea about a regular occupation. I been through so much. I never really had anything since my father went to prison. All I really want is just a basic job and a nice place to stay and provide for my son. I have a four year old son. I have his picture right here." He shows it to me, and smiles. "I'm married. Me and my wife are not together right now because of my incarceration. But we'll get back together again. Definitely."

Poor Simone, I think.

"Another thing I might add, all of this I did was petty stuff. Lots of times I went to jail because I had no place to go. A couple of times I did that. Just took some petty stuff so I could have a place to sleep.

JAMES

"If I had my way, I would cut myself off from the ways of America, of this racist society. I would even be my own black president. But whatever I do, would be entirely for black people."

He is a slim African American and always in black: black leather, black shirt, large black hat, dark sunglasses, dressed more for a bar than a soup kitchen. He is always alone and wears a sullen expression but, to my surprise, he asked to be interviewed. He is a mass of contradictions. He is arrogant and always punctuates his remarks with a firm, "All right!" He has intellectual aspirations and prides himself on his learning which is a strange mixture of half-truths and falsehoods with a strong taste for the ghoulish, though there are occasional flashes of insight. He is probably the most complicated, the most confused and possibly the most imaginative of the group.

When I was growing up, I could walk down the street and see the Milky Way, a big streak across the sky. It was like an everyday thing. But you don't see it now. Milky Way's gone. That beauty on earth is gone. I could walk down the street on a September night and the moon was bright white. All of a sudden, it was a deep, dark orange. Now you don't see that orange no more. And you don't see the Milky Way no more. Now you tell me why." (It sounds like a challenge or an accusation, as if I were somehow to blame.)

"Unfortunately I'm not doing nothin right now, which I'm not too happy about. But I have a lot of things to say. I did a lot which I'm not too proud of. But, you know, I was headstrong."

He is proud of his mother, a registered nurse, who worked at two jobs: at the hospital and also on private duty for University people who lived on Blackmore Avenue. "Where the University President lives," he added. "Her marriage, unfortunately, like most marriages in the black community, wasn't too good. You've got to be really fortunate to have a father that stays with you. I didn't see my father until I was fourteen."

There were three boys. James was in the middle. "My youngest brother was always closest to my mother, real close. He had a different father. His father didn't turn out too good either. But my mother did good by herself. Seemed to me my mother would do more for my elder brother than for me because he was a basketball star. But I think that was just the child's way. My mother fed me, clothed me, gave me a place to stay. What more could I want?" (Obviously, he wanted — and needed — a good deal more.) "I loved her," he insists. "Please God, she died two years ago. She was seventy.

"When I was, say, seven or eight years old, she would give me 25¢ for my school lunch and we used to go down to Warner's with the money and buy all these candies and play hookey. Or I would take that money — and the money I made as a shoeshine boy — and catch the bus and go to

Rockland, the amusement park. Didn't matter if we had enough money. We snuck in. It was more fun that way. My oldest brother saw us but he couldn't say nothing because what was *he* doing there? Mostly all the boys were doing the same thing. Except my youngest brother. He had more sense. He always went to school and then to college. He's a Correction Officer in Newark now."

In Junior High James played hookey so much that the school told his mother she had to bring him to school. He got a beating from her for that. He never resisted. "I don't care if I was twenty-one, she could beat me. I wouldn't put up a fight. I'd have to fight the whole family. We wouldn't dream of overpowering my mother. My stepfather, he was a big man, 6'4" and my mother was small. But one day, when my mother was still married to him, that man tried to overpower her. She picked up a telephone and he ended up with thirty-two stitches in his head."

Actually, James really liked school. His favorite study was astronomy. "Study of the planets and all that. I started astronomy when I was in the 3rd grade. I got to the point where you start using those encyclopedias. To this day, I can tell you how far almost any one of the planets is and how long it would take you to get there. Anthropology was another one. We didn't call it that. It was the study of dinosaurs and stuff like that. What was fascinating to me was the dinosaur display at the University Museum. And I developed a taste for Greek mythology from all those movies about Hercules. They didn't teach that in school but I learned about it from the library where they told us about Greek myths. I didn't understand a word but they had Hercules in there. I developed a liking for reading. I liked comic books. Even now, I'm reading classics. Even now, I'm on *The Odyssey.* Not in comics. I got it from the library. The Trojan horse, Helen of Troy and all that. Achilles, too. I started reading that kind of stuff in the

5th, 6th grade. I read at home a lot and I went to the library all the time. When I was younger, they had a library right there on Montgomery Street and you could go there and learn French. I learned how to count up to six. And I love history. I learned even though I wasn't in school very much. I like to read. You don't need a teacher if you can read.

"I read anything. I just finished a book about — what's that man's name — Jack the Ripper. All right. They had pictures of the way he cut these women up. I'm surprised that I didn't throw up my meal lookin at half of the pictures. But I'll read anything. Vampires are a weakness for me. Dracula is my idol. All right. I'm reading about vampires right now. Now a lot of mental wisdom tells me that that's a dangerous book to get into. I, myself, I don't see it like that. I'd much rather read it and get my own interpretations of it."

His mother made them all go to church. "So we could develop right from wrong." They went to the Community Baptist Church. They all sang in the choir and they all went to Sunday School. If James missed Sunday School, he had to go to the afternoon service. "I still go to church. My younger brother's writing for the church now. A newsletter. It's not a job. He has a genuine devotion for the Lord so he does it. I don't like to say I'm religious. I believe in God. I have a fear of God. I fear him enough to respect Him. But I'd never say I'm religious. I'm actually afraid to exalt myself in the name of the Lord by saying I'm religious and then going out there and doing something wrong. But I will say that I believe in Him and I fear Him enough to go to church. I fear Him enough not to do things that I shouldn't do."

He began to drink because of his stepfather. "I would see him sometimes when he was intoxicated and I would say to myself, why does he want to get like that? Why would anyone want to get like that? I started to drink just to see what it was like. We were all smoking and drinking at the age of ten. On promotion day, the teacher had a whole class room of drunken boys."

School was fighting, drinking, playing hookey, everything but education. The students were almost entirely black. "The Blacks were the racial problem. We were the trouble-makers. All the fighting was between Blacks. We had gangs but there was a lot of single fights, too. And if a white guy was unfortunate enough to be around, that was the end for him. You had to know how to fight. If you couldn't fight, you were in trouble. I had read *Manchild in the Promised Land.* Clyde Brown phrased it good. He said, 'When I was growing up, I was afraid *not* to fight.' When you think about it, that's the way it is. You were a manchild. You were actually a manchild at the age of ten or eleven."

James began to take drugs at the age of fifteen because an older friend was doing it and James was curious. It started with reefers, became heroin and LSD. He got the money by stealing. He also had a job washing dishes at Chuck's, a hamburger place. "But I could always come to work the next day. I never was strung out. Praise God, I never did get dependent on it to the point where I would wake up sick. Praise God." The others, he noticed, would drop a whole tablet of acid and get strung out. But he would drop a quarter. "I was fortunate. The Lord has spoken to me. The Lord has spoke.

"When I was very young, say about thirteen or fourteen, I got involved with the Black Panthers for a little while. I was one of them hippies. I wasn't into it officially but I got a lot of militant friends who were. They helped serve breakfast for the Panthers. That's the closest we got to politics. The Black Panthers were against drugs. You could not be a Black Panther if you were on drugs. They said, 'You talk about you hate Whitey, yet you're shooting the worst weapon they could come up with. And you're killing each other. I mean, why go ahead and say you're for black people when you're shooting drugs yourself or selling it to them?' A lot of this took with me. But I didn't stay away from drugs. It was too late."

He was sent to the Juvenile Detention Center many times for stealing, but only stayed overnight once. "That was during a riot. I was lootin stuff and I was caught. All right. It was like a Boys' Home. I played games, I ate, I went to bed. I stayed overnight and the next day my mother came, took me home and gave me a beating. I had to go to Juvenile Court. They let me go but they gave me a warning which I didn't listen to and the next time I ended up on probation for about a year. That's the only time I got punished. I pride myself on that."

He stole because he liked to steal, not to support his habit. "I didn't have a habit. I was a thief because, believe it or not, it was fun. And the other boys were doing it. Sometimes I robbed with the group, sometimes by myself. I only robbed stores. I never robbed people. I robbed cameras, stuff like that, and sold it to stores. They didn't care where I got it. I got caught a lot. But I was lucky. Nothing really stuck to me. Nothing to convict me."

He tried going to the Skill Center. He was paid to go and he wanted the money. "You went like you went to school, eight hours a day. I only liked it for the people. It wasn't so much me learning anything as me fuckin off. (He stopped suddenly and turned to the tape.) "Oh, excuse me."

He was eighteen and wondering what would happen to him without a high school diploma. He quit his job because they weren't paying him enough and went to night school. He also started going to church and got a job at the Knights of Columbus as a dishwasher. He was feeling good about himself. He was doing the right thing. "One day the cops came to my house and arrested me for something I did three months ago. Someone snitched. That's why I like to do things by myself."

He had to go to jail while waiting to be tried. He had a good time there because he knew half the people so he didn't have to worry about being molested or attacked. Before the trial, he had his pastor phone the court and tell them he was going to night school, was working, and was going to church quite regularly. "So, when they saw all that on the record, they said, 'This guy's trying to get himself together.' That saved me. They were right. That was my last hit. I was eighteen. I don't know what changed my mind. I think, one day I said, 'I'm tired of this.' Let's say, I just grew up."

He finished night school in three years. "They even had a graduation so I ended up in a cap and gown. That was my dream. My mother was there. She saw me graduate. She was pleased. I was twenty-three."

He enlisted in the Navy to see what it was like, to get away from New Hope and to travel. He was in for four years. "I got along with the Whites as well as the Blacks. Everybody else did, too. We had fun. Go ashore. All those chicks. We went all over the place. I loved it.

"Paris was having trouble with the Communists. Every place got some kind of prejudice. You take Egypt. There's prejudice there but it's different than here. Ours comes from color. Theirs is more religious. In Paris, France, England, it's not a racial thing, or a religious thing but more like a political thing. All right.

"England was good. I met a young lady and she showed me the sights. It was beautiful. I liked getting away from America. The people in England don't have the prejudice like the people here. Prejudice there was based on how much money you had, how much prestige you had. All right. If you was all right, you got to go. If you wasn't, that's too bad. Whereas here, I don't care how much money you've got, your skin means a lot. England wasn't like that.

"I didn't stay in the Navy. The Navy wasn't me. I got married after I got out. But marriage wasn't me either. I didn't want to be with my wife and I began drinking heavily to more or less compensate. Which also messed me up at the job. I tried to get help but it was too late. So now I'm starting to tell about my incline. I mean my decline.

"The Lord says marriage is a sacred thing and divorce is a sin. Well, if that's the case, if I got to be around her and be miserable all my life just to please God — and God knows I believe in God — then I have to sin. I gotta be me. I gotta be the one to please myself. All right.

"I love museums and I love to go back in time. I love the kind of things that mystify me. I'm really into the occult. All right. I loved Stonehenge, wondering how these here rocks was able to stand all this time because they don't have no foundation known to man. I'm into things like Merlin, the magician. I don't know if the man was real. Me, myself, I figure that he was a man with a profound knowledge.

"The same thing with Jesus Christ. I believe in God. All right. I believe in God because I'm a Baptist. Now my church believes with the Trinity. I can't go along with that because there's too much dispute against it. And I don't believe in Jesus as a Savior so much as I believe in him as a man who has so much knowledge about God or relating to God that people had to listen to him. Like I do with Merlin, with witchcraft, with the devil. But I ain't gonna say that Jesus is God. I'll call him a prophet. I believe that he might have been sent. But the same thing goes for Buddha and his race. The same thing goes for Mohammed and Islam. The same thing goes for everybody else. All right.

"I never join anything. I was brought up in the Panthers but I didn't join them. I dug where they were coming from but I don't believe in organizations. I don't believe in causes. If it coincides with what I believe in, I'll go with it. But I don't join. I don't believe in commitment. In the Navy, I never committed myself. I never committed myself even to marriage.

OK! I don't commit myself to nothin. I'm keeping myself to myself.

"There's a conspiracy against black people. I don't know why. I've seen pictures of the man who taught Kit Carson. If you ever heard of him at all, or saw his pictures, you'd think he was white. I went a little bit deeper and found the man was black. I found out here in the library. Reading is a virtue and knowledge is a virtue. Also, take the Bible. Moses was of black skin. Because if he wasn't, that Pharaoh would say, 'Hey, this man ain't no Egyptian.'

"I just got on the City (Welfare) and I'm at the Y now. It's all right long as you mind your own business. Discreetness is a value to me. I'm very high on discreetness. I don't want too many people knowing what I'm doing.

"The soup kitchen is better than nothing. All right! I'd likc to do much better but right now it's the best I can do so I do it, you know? I don't hate to go. There are a lot of people I grew up with there. But — I stay to myself. People come around and they talk and chat. It's all right.

"I go to the museums. Saturdays I like to go to the Art Museum, check out the movie they're showing. I go to the Natural History Museum, the Colonial Museum. I love the library. Sometimes I go to Bennett Wharf because on Saturday they've got these here free boat rides. You'll go with me next Saturday, won't you? And the museum too, sometime. Sure you will." (It is more of a challenge than an invitation.)

"I've tried to find work but it hasn't been successful. But soon as I can find me a job, I'll be going back to New York. I enjoy the luxuries of New York: National Museum of Science, Jazz Museum. I been to New York a lotta times. I got a brother there but I don't know where.

"I'm not on drugs now. I stopped because I figured there was something better to do. Wasn't hard to stop. Anybody can do it. All right. I knew this man who told me something that stuck with me. Whatever you were born with, you can't change. You were born needing to eat and drink. You have to do that. You wasn't born with a cigarette in your mouth. You wasn't born with a spike in your arm. If you're determined to stop, you don't have to go to no program. I stopped a couple of months ago because I was tired of it. I mean, I been doing drugs since I was fifteen. All right. I had to stop sometime. I got myself checked up. I don't have no AIDS, no disease. Nothing like that. Lotta my friends are dead now — from AIDS. I'd say from life.

"I would like to take New Hope back to what it was once. With the movie houses, skating rinks, things like that. I will build up Montgomery Avenue again, the way it was when I grew up. It wasn't nice, but it was blackness. There was a unity. That unity was a black power struggle. It's black now but the unity's gone. You don't see that black power struggle no more. They watching TV instead. OK. That's manipulation.

"I would like to own a whole street with a barber shop, a furniture store, a clothing store, a food market, everything. All right. And maybe a couple of movie houses and a black studio, like a black Hollywood. Just for Blacks with no dependence on the white man whatsoever. We wouldn't have to worry about the mayor cutting off the library funds. If I had my way, I would cut myself off from the ways of America, from this racist society. I would even be my own black president. But whatever I do, is going to be entirely for black people. I'm friends with everybody. Everybody can sit down and talk to me. But my love is to my people. Whatever I do, that's for them.

"I don't say my society's gonna be better than the white society. I don't say it's gonna be different. I was brought up with the American culture, which means that the way I'm thinking would be based on the American culture. I'm gonna tell you something right now. Out of all the societies in the world, wasn't no society ever more dominant or more powerful than the American society. And it's the youngest country in existence. I'm talking about dominance, super-power. All right! So my society, it wouldn't be too much different. There'd be rich and poor. If you're smart enough to make money, then I say go and get it.

"I'm not here to change the world. I'm just here to change my life. There's a lot of things I would have done differently but it's too late to cry over spilled milk. I don't regret anything I did. All right!"

MARK

"If I'm a judge, maybe I could actually do something to help these juvenile drug dealers."

He is seventeen but looks much younger, a gentle-looking African American with a soft voice and a shy, very sober manner. He rarely smiles and then only fleetingly. It may be that he considers smiling inappropriate in a soup kitchen. He is always neatly dressed in a black jacket and black cap with its peak up front. He is very intelligent and his speech is quite literate but when talking about his school or his friends, he lapses into ghetto talk. He comes to the soup kitchen with his father and they are always together, aloof from the others. His father, a short, plump man with a round face, smiles a good deal, perhaps to make up for his son who smiles so little. They have been in New Hope for less than a year. This may be what gives Mark that slightly detached air, as if he really belongs somewhere else. They are devout Muslims.

I'm not in school right now. I stopped going in my sophomore year." His mother and sister still live in New York where he grew up. He went to a Muslim elementary school there. Boys and girls were in the same classroom but, outside, the girls played with the girls and the boys with the boys. The girls had their hair all covered and wore traditional clothes. The boys wore loose-fitting pants and loose-fitting shirts. "It was like a uniform so there couldn't be any differences. It didn't make me self-conscious because I'm proud to be a Muslim." But when he got home, he changed into western clothes.

"The school was, basically, good but it had a lot of discipline. They taught you how to share." One day one of "the brothers" wanted Mark's piece of cake. When Mark refused to give it to him, the teacher took him to a room in the basement and beat him with a big paddle. That was in kindergarten. The beatings got harder as he got older. But he was stubborn. In about the 3rd grade, he learned. He has even come to believe in the justice of the beatings.

When he was in the 8th grade, the family moved farther downtown, to Madison City on the lower East Side so his mother could be closer to her job. "My mother has a good job as a computer engineer with a television station. My father was a chauffeur for a limousine company. He drove people to motels and offices and airports and kids home from their fancy boarding schools — in a Mercedes-Benz. He took me to the Mosque every Friday. They had activities, games, plays. I liked that. But we moved away, near 13th Street where the L train stops." His more or less peaceful life stopped as well.

The tenants there were predominantly black. "It looked all right from the outside. No one was out on the street selling drugs for nickels and dimes like here. They were selling it *inside,* whole bags of it — by weight. The parents were inside too, getting stoned. It was the sons who were dealing."

The school was two blocks away, a mass of brick behind a high fence. "It was supposed to be the best in the neighborhood. Best at fighting, I guess. Weren't any Muslims there. A few Puerto Ricans. A few Whites but they wouldn't even come to school. It was too dangerous. So the Blacks formed gangs and fought each other."

Mark was never really a member of any gang but he had lots of friends. "Either you have friends or you don't. Your friends are your people. You fight with them, you eat with them, you be with them. If I got into any kind of violence, my friends would make sure that nothing ever happened to me. People that weren't hanging with any gang were almost like rejected. They would be in danger of getting robbed and beaten up. In the beginning, they just beat up on people with sticks and baseball bats. Then, in about the 10th or 11th grade, it was knives — and then guns. 8th and 9th grade fight each other; 10th and 11th grade fight each other. And then everybody fights everybody. There was so much fighting it was like part of the school routine, like recess or math or lunch. Somebody would get beat up with a stick, somebody would get stabbed, somebody would get shot." In the upper grades, the boys brought guns right into the school. The girls carried them in. No one ever searched the girls. "It was Black on Black. Blacks fighting each other. No wonder people said in another ten years, black men would be extinct.

"Only thing you learned in school was how to survive, how to be tough, how to steal, rob, sell drugs. How to fight, how to beat people with sticks, how to stab people, how to shoot people. It was almost like a school for criminals. Because in school was no playing. If they say, 'I'll beat you down at that school,' they're gonna do it. If you run home, they're gonna come to your house and beat you there."

There was no one who felt as he did, no one he could talk to. His mother had chosen that environment for him so she could be closer to her job. "My father might want to help but what could he do? Just smile and say, 'Be patient, boy. You gotta have patience.'" He was a man who spent his life being patient, sitting in a car, waiting: for the lights to change, the traffic to move, the clients to appear. As for the people in church, Mark could not even talk to them. "If they knew the kind of friends I had, I would be severely punished. But if I didn't have them, I would be in real trouble.

"I had to situate myself from their activities. I pulled a few fights but I never really got into that routine because I've got a lot of will power from my religion. When I first started getting down with them, they tried to put me through a test to see where I was at."

He was going home one day when Skeetch and a crowd of boys carrying sticks and bats surrounded him in the schoolyard. "'Time you was tested,' Skeetch told me. 'So we can see where you're at. Everybody gets tested. I don't know how come we waited on you so long.'

'Tested? How?'

'I'm comin to that.' He stuck his face into mine." They were going to rob a jewelry store with Mark as front man. "'He give you any problems, you jes use one of these,' Skeetch said. He patted the gun in his pocket.

"For Muslims, stealing and killing are sins. If you steal, you get your right hand cut off. If you kill, you die. That's the law of Koran. Didn't matter that it wasn't the law for those kids. It was *my* law. And it was *God's* law. 'I'm not doin it,' I told them. 'I'm not goin out there with no sticks and no baseball bat an no gun. I'm not doin it.'

"Skeetch got mad. 'Look like we're gonna have to shoot him right now,' he said. 'That way we know he ain't gonna snitch.'

"I wasn't worried about getting hurt. I figure that's just another phase of life. Besides, Koran says, 'What hit you couldn't have missed you, what missed you couldn't have hit you.' If God wanted me to die, I would die. If not, I would live. Wasn't up to Skeetch. He was nothing but a punk, a punk with a gun. 'Get outta my face,' I told him. 'You wanna shoot me, shoot me. I can die right now. No matter what you do to this body, it's just a shell. But if you shoot me, you're goin to jail. I'm not gonna steal and beat up on somebody and shoot somebody and then go to jail with you. What you gonna do in jail? Sit around and smoke and talk shit? Save that for somebody else. I'm goin home.'

'You ain't goin nowhere,' Skeetch told me.

"Then Cube shouted from the back of the crowd, 'Leave him alone.' He was a real tight friend. He was older and he was pretty cool. We called him Cube for Ice Cube. He liked my sister so, basically, he was my personal protector.

'Man, what makes Mark so special?' Skeetch said. 'He hangin out with us and then, when it's time to prove hisself, he don't wanna do nothin. Man, let's beat this nigger down.'

'You got a hearin problem, man?' Cube said. 'I tole you, leave him alone. I'm messin with his sister. So you jes leave him alone.'

"But I didn't need any protection. I'm not afraid to die. Because living like this is dying. Most of the students in that school were punks, pussies. They couldn't stand up for themselves. If anyone said, 'Sell these drugs, man,' they'd all go out and sell them. Just because they were afraid not to. It was like a school for drug dealers." That was something everyone could learn to do. And almost everyone did. Even Cube.

"'Man,' Cube said, 'we all playin the white man's game, the materialistic game. We strive for these things we want but we can't never have them.

Because anything you want, you gotta pay for. You gotta pay taxes on your house, you gotta pay taxes on your car, you gotta pay taxes on your life. You get old, they give you a social security number. You go to jail, they give you another number. All you is is a number, man. You walking around here like a statistic. OK, I'm gonna be a nice, big, high statistic. I'm gonna sell these drugs, I'm gonna make this money and I'm gonna drive that Porsche.'

'An you'll still be playin the white man's game,' I told him. 'Only you can't win. You'll kill yourself selling that stuff, man. When you get arrested, you think they gonna come get you outta jail? They'll leave you in there. You gonna do it by yourself. Like you took that package by yourself. You run that block by yourself. And you be in that jail by yourself. Doin time. *By yourself.* That's the reality of it.'

"Not many Muslims in the drug trade because in Muslim society, if you take a life, it's death. That's the rule of Koran. If you're selling drugs, that's death because you're killing somebody — slowly. If you're taking drugs, you're killing yourself. You're destroying your brain and your will power and you're preventing everything God believes in, everything He put you on this earth to do. To be. In Koran, God says, 'Do not come before me befuddled in the brain.'"

Tonk, Mark's best friend, was arrested for selling drugs. When he came out of prison, he went right back to dealing again. "'Don't do it,' I told him. 'Because how long you gonna keep that money? You'll get busted again — you know you will — and again. And lose it all. And each time, you'll be in jail longer. And each time you'll be worrying about somebody gonna kick your butt or beat you up or even kill you — in or out of jail.'"

But Mark knows it wasn't only his will power or even his religion that kept him from selling drugs. "Why would I sell drugs? My parents would buy me anything I wanted. But Tonk, like most of the other kids, had to deal because their mothers were doing drugs and putting them through a lot of changes. They were basically from poor families. And once you start dealing, you can't stop. They won't let you.

"The teachers were basically scared of the students. Like one day in the middle of science class, the teacher was explaining something and a kid said, 'I don't wanna do this shit.' And that was the end of that science class. This happened in other classes, too. Kids went to sleep in the classroom, even had sex in class — in the closets. If you wanted to learn anything, you had to go to the library and look it up for yourself. Teach yourself."

One day, Devereaux, a big hunk of a show-off, began to draw penises and vaginas all over the blackboard. "Mr. Rankin, the teacher, a real cool guy, got pissed off, grabbed him and banged his head against the board. Deveraux pulled out a knife and stabbed him. But he didn't really hurt him. It was only a little knife.

"One day Devereaux came to class with a gun in his hand and said, 'Don't nobody move. This just gonna be for Skeetch cause he been cuttin into my territory. Don't nobody do that an live. But anybody start actin funny, I could get nervous and shoot a few other people, too.'

"Skeetch jumped up, ran into the hall and headed for his locker. He kept his gun and all his friends' guns, about ten of them, stashed away in there. He was going to hand them out and shoot it out with Devereaux right there in the hall. Meanwhile, the teacher was shouting into the intercom that there was a boy on the third floor with a gun. The guards caught Devereaux as he was running down the stairs. They caught Skeetch, too. All the boys who owned guns were expelled.

"I wasn't expelled. I didn't own a gun. But I left anyway." Though he wasn't a real member of the gang, he had been hanging out with them.

They were his friends. Besides, he wasn't learning anything in school and it was getting increasingly dangerous. So, at fifteen, he dropped out — without his parent's knowledge. At sixteen, he signed himself out for good.

The drug war was on in full force now. "Wasn't ever any real war *against* drugs, only *for* drugs." One afternoon, a week later, Skeetch was shot down on the street with his gun still in his pocket. Tonk's boss was attacked by a rival dealer and two of his workers were killed. One of them was Tonk. "The boys that killed Tonk boasted they were gonna kill me, too.They were gonna kill *all* Tonk's friends."

By then, Mark's parents had decided to separate. Mark chose to go with his father. "In a way, maybe I did the right thing. Like that male bonding thing. But then, in another way, maybe I didn't. With my mother, I could have been more financially secure. But maybe with my father, I'm learning something more valuable: experience of life. We get along. We basically understand each other."

Mark's father decided to move to New Hope where Mark would be safe from drugs and bullets and where there would be lots of jobs for him. "My father said there wasn't any recession in New Hope because they make guns there and people are always wanting guns." But there *was* a recession in New Hope. Black men gathered in front of derelict stores or sat on benches in the park or pushed grocery carts piled with trash bags and rubbish, through the streets. "Looked like collecting used bottles and cans for a nickel a piece was the biggest industry in town," Mark said.

Instead of work, Mark and his father found Welfare and the soup kitchens and a two-room apartment on Button Street in the ghetto where the litter grows knee-high and drugs flourish on the corners. People are shot almost every day, just for being there. Old women sit locked in their apartments in terror. Stray bullets killed a young girl, coming out of her house, a boy sitting on his front porch, a child in a pram. Just to walk to the corner was an act of courage — or folly.

"Button Street is even worse than Madison City and the kids are even dumber," Mark said, "because they're actually *out* there selling nickels' and dimes' worth of cocaine right on the street. Right out where you're stepping on other dealers' toes, where you could actually get dropped by shooters or people walking up to you and beating your brains out. And then you have to worry about the police running after you. There's so many things you've got to think about when you start selling drugs.

"I wouldn't ever consider having these kid for my friends. They're too wild. They've lost all respect for human life. If I have to fight those psychopaths, I'll fight them, but, basically, I want to situate myself away from them." He stays in the house and reads or goes to the library to watch video tapes or borrow books. "Anything that has to do, basically, with drugs and juveniles. I want to know why kids use drugs, why they sell drugs, why they murder people and gang bang. What's the sense in it?"

He has a library card that he always keeps in a little wallet in his pocket. "So if the police actually grab me and think I was doing something illegal, I'll show it to them and tell them, 'No, it wasn't me.'"

Mark and his father have no friends or relatives in town. And after seven months, they still have not found work. They pray together every night. Then they sit on the floor on their mattresses with their backs against the wall and talk. Mark's father teaches him about shopping — how to read labels and look for bargains — and Mark tells him about the books he is reading on cocaine and its effects. "It's terrible stuff. Makes you irrational, violent. You do anything to get it: rob, stab, shoot. The drug dulls the reasoning part of your brain so you lose all control. I don't know an awful lot yet but I want to find out as much as I can."

He would like to be a judge. Then he could make decisions about juvenile drug dealers. "They aren't all bad. They're just doing what the environment calls for. It's the only way they can survive. And for you to punish someone for trying to survive is insane. Besides, *dealing* drugs is an addiction, just like *doing* drugs. Because the money and the lifestyle is real fast-paced and you can get addicted to that just like on a high. You've got to scare it out of them. Bring them up hard. I'd talk to them, find out where they're coming from. If they're the greedy, violent type, I'd throw them in the jug. Let them sit there for a while. But if they were decent and wanted to change, I'd get some kind of program going for them. Put them on probation. Help them find some other way to survive. If I'm a judge, they would have to do what I say, wouldn't they?"

He would like to go back to school. "There was a lady in the library yesterday said she would give me a chance to get my GED. I wouldn't graduate with a cap and gown but I would get my diploma." After that he might get a scholarship to some college out of town, away from the city. "Then I could come back and be a judge. If I'm a judge, maybe I could actually do something to help these juvenile drug dealers.

"God put you on this earth to do something positive for somebody. Maybe I was put here to do something about *them.*"

EPILOGUE

EPILOGUE

It is several years later and most of the voices recorded here have faded away, except for the occasional echoes inside my head. I hear them at odd times during the day with all their individual accents, inflections and emotions.

In 1818, the State Constitution made it obligatory for the State to provide food, clothing and shelter for all its citizens, a law that has been steadily disregarded. Recently, the cuts in Welfare that the homeless so dreaded, were enacted. Shelters were closed and the few that remained charged $3.00 a night. The war against poverty had become a war against the poor.

PEOPLE FIRST camped on the New Hope Green in protest, but were evicted — even from their tents. I no longer see the homeless on the streets or in the Mall or on the Green or in Columbus Park which has been completely refurbished. It now has a drinking fountain, elegant Victorian lamps and new benches with arm rests down the center to keep anyone from sleeping there. It has not made that impossible, only much more uncomfortable, and I have occasionally seen a homeless man hunched up on one of the benches. But where are the others? Have they been removed from the streets and sent to jail to avoid offending the public? The poor may not hate the rich but the evidence suggests that the rich hate the poor.

Yet PEOPLE FIRST went on to expand the hours of their Day Center which is open seven days a week now and they have hopes of expanding their services as well to include a clinic, a literacy program, a worker-owner temporary labor center, a youth program and a housing program.

The soup kitchens are still crowded, mostly with new faces, though I still see some familiar ones around town. I met Conrad of the big smile and the "Don't play politics with the food, man," pushing a cart full of trash bags down the street. He was so thin I did not recognize him until he hailed me. He has been living in a cave in the park. "It's okay," he said, reassuringly. "I have a heater so I manage to keep pretty warm."

Paul, who needed new teeth and a haircut, stopped coming to the soup kitchen last year. Recently I saw him again, sitting alone on a bench near my house looking very tired and very shabby with long hair and a long beard. Evidently he never got that haircut or that new set of teeth. He was surprised and pleased when I greeted him. "You remembered my name!" he said. He was evicted from his room when his rent subsidy was cut and was forced to go to a shelter. But the shelter closed and now he lives in the street. He sleeps on benches, which he claims are warmer than the ground. "I love to look at the grass and the squirrels," he said. "Did you know there are squirrels with red tails?" He told me about a trip he once took to Italy. "I love Rome, art, Michelangelo." I asked him several times why he stopped coming to the soup kitchens. "Because I'm ashamed," he said at last. I offered him money for food which he refused. "I don't want to eat," he said. "And I don't need money. The local grocery store lets me have cigarettes on credit." I managed to force a blanket on him, though he was worried about how he could return it. When I left, he smiled. "It was so nice talking to you," he said.

I saw him again, much later, on the Green. He looked quite different. He still needs new teeth but his beard was gone and his hair was cut. He's living in a room now. "I'm fine," he said, "just fine."

Walking downtown one spring morning, I heard someone call, "Is it time for seconds yet?" It was Alex, the reformed alcoholic, wearing white trousers and a white turtleneck and looking extremely pleased. He's working as a nurse's aid at the VA hospital. "I don't need the soup kitchen anymore," he said proudly.

Muriel, the homeless woman, greeted me in the supermarket one morning. She looked somewhat better with her hair combed and without her plastic shopping bags. She obviously felt much better for, unpredictable as ever, she threw her arms around me and said how glad she was to see me and told me what a good friend I was. She is living in a room now, thanks to the efforts of Kate and the Jefferson House Outreach Program.

Julian, of the suitcase with a filing system, was sitting in the sun on the steps of the Congregational Church one morning. He has a permanent job with the church now and plans are underway to start a newspaper for the homeless, like *The Big Issue* in England and the newspaper of the Partnership of the Homeless in New York. He is quite excited about it and expects to edit and write for it. But though I have been watching for it, I haven't, as yet, seen it anywhere.

Deirdre arrived at the soup kitchen very late one night after a long absence. She was not wearing any bandages but she seemed more disconnected and remote than ever. Our food was all gone, which did not seem to upset her, but she wanted a ride home. The last time I drove her home, it was to the YWCA. This time she sent me in a totally different direction. "I just Pine Sol'd the whole place," she said. "Peg was furious at the smell." After a moment, I realized that she was referring to Pine Sol, a household disinfectant, and that Peg must be her roommate. Which means, I thought happily, that she finally has a room.

We stopped at an abandoned department store. "Come and see how the homeless live," she said. We picked our way, with the aid of her flashlight, across a dark, paved area covered with litter and puddles and smelling of urine. "In there," Deirdre said. It was a bare, recessed, paved section beneath the building, with one whole side open to the street. Was this what she had "Pine Sol'd?" "A huge board was propped across the opening, far too heavy for us to move but over it I could see a woman lying in the far corner. "Peg," Deirdre shouted, playing the flashlight on her face. "Peg! Peg, let me in." But the woman did not move. Deirdre kept shouting more and more frantically and waving the flashlight in Peg's face. But still she did not stir. I was beginning to feel worried. There had been a story in the paper that morning of a man found frozen to death on the Green. "Peg's a diabetic," Deirdre said, between shouts and sobs. She may be in a diabetic coma, I thought, with a feeling of panic. She may be dead already.

I left Deirdre and ran down the streets looking for an emergency telephone. By the time I got back, two patrol cars and two ambulances were already parked in front of the building with enormous floodlights shining on the entire area. Peg, a huge woman, was leaning over the board. "Get those fuckin lights off me!" she shouted furiously.

I apologized to the police and the paramedics who were extremely good-natured and said it happened all the time. They agreed that Deirdre's "home" was "terrible" but they sounded more disgusted than horrified. "How can these people live like that?" they said, as if "these people" had a choice.

Driving home, I wondered if Peg would refuse to let Deidre into their "Pine Sol'd room" to punish her for calling the police; and realized, suddenly, how cold I was.

Cliffie, big, childish, effusive Cliffie, no longer asks me for a ride home for he no longer comes to the soup kitchen. He was found dead on the floor of his room with half a bottle of Jim Beam and a trash bag full of "empties" beside him. Harper read his obituary in the soup kitchen one evening just before grace. The paper told us almost nothing but his full name, which was Clifford Clarence Tiff, his age and his surviving relatives. It was a surprise to learn that he *had* relatives: sisters and brothers and uncles and aunts who lived right here in town, and even a mother and *two* fathers. Cliffie had never mentioned them, never seemed to go to them for money or help of any kind. It was a surprise, too, to learn that he was thirty-seven. A few of us from the soup kitchens went to the funeral. I wanted to see Cliffie home for the last time.

The small chapel was almost full with men in dark suits and women in flowing dresses and enormous hats like upside-down baskets, sobbing into wads of tissue. I wondered who all those prosperous-looking people were who had waited for Cliffie to die before acknowledging him.

At the front of the chapel, two huge vases of bold-looking flowers stood guard at either end of the open coffin. Cliffie was at last, as he always longed to be, the center of attention. He was stretched out on a frilly, satin lining in a dark suit, a crisp, white shirt and striped tie. His fingernails were polished, his head was uncovered and his hair was smooth as a well-laid rug. He looked portly rather than plump and much older. He wasn't Cliffie anymore. He was Clifford now. He had grown up at last.

A few of the former guests still come to the soup kitchen, sometimes just to say "hello." Walter, the reader and linguist, comes only occasionally as he is afraid of gaining weight. He still reads voraciously in the University library, goes to free concerts at the University and is attending a series of lectures on astronomy. "I'm re-reading Condorcet," he said with a smile before I had a chance to ask him. "I've always liked the Enlightenment."

Spike, once so loud, so jovial, who sang over the huge pots and pans, came very rarely for a while — and very late. We had found an apartment for him at last, but he no longer lives there. When he came to the kitchen, he wandered around the back of the room, did not say "hello," ate nothing, and sat with his head down and a stunned expression. Finally he stopped coming entirely. One night he showed up again and seemed restored to his old self. He gave me his old, exuberant greeting and his old bear hug. He was just out of the hospital, he said, where he had been treated for depression. When I asked if it helped, he said, "Don't help when I gotta go back to the same ole pressures: my girl doin me in and me not gettin my Compensation and men wantin to kill me."

Al, the Green Beret veteran, who spent his days in the library with a computer working on proposals for his new business and his evenings in the soup kitchens, cooking and making rousing speeches against the cuts, has disappeared from both places. I heard he had gone back to the VA hospital for treatment as he planned. But that was a time long ago.

Recently, I met James who dreamed of an all-black society with himself as president. He looked quite trim in a trenchcoat and khaki trousers. He was on his way to the hospital to begin his drug treatment. I congratulated him warmly. "You'll come visit me, won't you?" he said. I agreed but we both forgot that I did not know his last name.

I had compiled a list of drug rehabilitation programs for Michelle, the young prostitute, but she did not come to the soup kitchen for a long time after our interview. She finally turned up one evening looking entirely different in a white blouse, black skirt, high-heeled shoes and no hat. We hugged and I told her she looked marvelous, which she did. But I wondered what this drastic change could mean. Luckily, a drug counselor was in the kitchen that evening and Michelle was quite willing to talk to her. I introduced them, they sat down together, away from the others, and spent the rest of the evening talking. They were still there when I left. I have no idea what the outcome was. Michelle has not been back to the kitchen since.

Josie, who was always "starting over," has a new boyfriend now. "He's real nice," she said. Her former boyfriend, Ray, went back to drugs and drink right after the cuts. Just as he said he would. He never comes to the soup kitchen anymore and is no longer involved with PEOPLE FIRST. "He's too ashamed," Josie said. If so, what a waste. He was a dedicated worker for the homeless. But perhaps he is living a happy and useful life somewhere else.

Josie came a few times after that, then disappeared. Starting over, I thought and hoped that somewhere, somehow, she had a nice place to live and had her children back and was happy.

Eric, the industrial engineer, came occasionally for a while. His arthritis has evidently grown worse for, standing or walking, he seemed to be in considerable pain. Yet he always carried a heavy load with him: books, art portfolios, several plastic bags and a large backpack. I was told that he had lost his room and moved to a shelter. The last time I saw him, he was rummaging through a trash can. I tried to decide which would be less humiliating to him: to offer him money or to leave him to pick around in the trash, unseen. In the end, I walked by, careful not to let him see me. By the time I turned the corner, I decided it was the wrong choice. I went back but he was no longer there.

I still meet Kenneth, the pianist, on the street and in the library. He will be playing a solo part in a concert in New York in the spring and expects to do two more in the fall. He was given an electric piano with headphones so that he can practice without disturbing his neighbors, has acquired several new students, and has a part-time appointment at the Wells School of Music. He is as buoyant as ever and expects to get new teeth soon.

Morgan, the ex-railroad man, is a railroad man again. He telephoned me from Arizona where he has a job as a conductor on a passenger train. Later, he sent me a photograph of himself in uniform, standing beside his train. I could almost hear his loud, cheerful voice shouting, "All Aboard."

But, for most of the guests, there is no train waiting in sunny Arizona. There are only the long lines of the soup kitchen moving slowly, night after night, and the long, cold winter ahead. Driving home after the kitchen closed, I see the guests walking down the dark, windy streets, carrying their soup kitchen "take outs" in blue *New York Times* plastic bags, going "home" — to an apartment, a room, a bed, a park bench, a piece of grass, a slab of cement.

"Tonight will be very cold and very windy," my car radio announces, "with the temperature dropping to below zero and a wind chill factor of ten below. Snow, which will start around midnight, is expected to reach from eight to ten inches." I think of Paul and Muriel and Deirdre and Josie and Julian and Kenneth and Ray and all the others who were forced, at one time or another, or even permanently, to live on the streets of this city — a city named so proudly by its founders, New Hope.